Writing Simple Poems

CAMBRIDGE HANDBOOKS FOR LANGUAGE TEACHERS

This is a series of practical guides for teachers of English and other languages. Illustrative examples are usually drawn from the field of English as a foreign or second language, but the ideas and techniques described can equally well be used in the teaching of any language.

In this series:

Writing Simple Poems

Pattern Poetry
for Language Acquisition

Vicki L. Holmes

and

Margaret R. Moulton

CAMBRIDGE
UNIVERSITY PRESS

PUBLISHED BY THE PRESS SYNDICATE OF THE UNIVERSITY OF CAMBRIDGE
The Pitt Building, Trumpington Street, Cambridge, United Kingdom

CAMBRIDGE UNIVERSITY PRESS
The Edinburgh Building, Cambridge CB2 2RU, UK
40 West 20th Street, New York, NY 10011-4211, USA
10 Stamford Road, Oakleigh, VIC 3166, Australia
Ruiz de Alarcón 13, 28014 Madrid, Spain
Dock House, The Waterfront, Cape Town 8001, South Africa

http://www.cambridge.org

First published 2001

Printed in the United States of America

Typeface Sabon 10½/12 pt.

A catalog record for this book is available from the British Library

Library of Congress Cataloging-in-Publication Data

Holmes, Vicki L.
Writing simple poems : pattern poetry for language acquisition / Vicki L. Holmes,
Margaret R. Moulton.
p. cm. – (Cambridge handbooks for language teachers)
Includes bibliographical references and index.
ISBN 0-521-78552-9
I. Moulton, Margaret R.   II. Title.   III. Series.

PE1128.A2 H65 2001
808.1 – dc21   00-052919

ISBN 0 521 785529 paperback

Contents

Contents

Acknowledgments

This book would not have been possible without the help of many fine teachers (and their students), who either taught some of these lessons and sent their students' poems to us or allowed us to come into their classrooms and test the lessons ourselves. These teachers gave us many good suggestions for changes, and their students' responses were both gratifying and helpful. We would, therefore, like to thank these teachers, their students, and their schools. The following schools took on our poetry-writing project as projects of their own:

Gene Ward Elementary School, Las Vegas, Nevada
   Pat Hodges, principal
   Maria Chavez, assistant principal
   Elizabeth Gordon Taylor, teacher
   Ruth Devlin, teacher
John S. Park Elementary School, Las Vegas, Nevada
   Linda Agreda, principal
   Karen Callahan, teacher
   Carrie Shatraw, teacher
   Angie Soares, teacher
William E. Orr Middle School, Las Vegas, Nevada
   Barbara Rosenberg, principal
   Pat Arroyo, teacher
   Lance Egan, teacher
   Sybil Raimon, teacher
Las Vegas High School, Las Vegas, Nevada
   Barry Gunderson, principal
   Claudette Willems, teacher
   Joannie Monroy, teacher

Other teachers individually volunteered to write poems with their students:

Jennifer Drao, Mike O'Callaghan Middle School, Las Vegas, Nevada
Amber James (student teacher), Helen Cannon Middle School, Las Vegas, Nevada
Christina O'Neal, Elizabeth Wilhelm Elementary School, Las Vegas, Nevada
Sandra Smith, Chinle Junior High School, Chinle, Arizona

Acknowledgments

John Streusik, Clark County School District Adult Education Program, Las Vegas, Nevada

Jean Mauer, English Language Center, University of Nevada, Las Vegas

Still other teachers also helped us in years past by experimenting with the poems before we even knew we would write this book. We thank them for sharing their students' poems, thereby encouraging us to pursue our project and share it with even more teachers and students. We would also like to thank our administrators at the University of Nevada, Las Vegas, who provided us with support and time to work on this project:

Jim Frey, Dean of the College of Liberal Arts
Gene Hall, Dean of the College of Education
Jane McCarthy, Chair of the Department of Curriculum and Instruction

Finally, we would like to thank our editor at Cambridge University Press, Penny Ur, for her valuable suggestions, encouraging comments, and timely responses, allowing us to improve both our lessons and our writing.

Writing Simple Poems

Introduction

Why we wrote this book

As English teachers, we struggled for years with ways to reinforce grammar points in our lessons. We tried drills, worksheets, cloze exercises, and a host of other traditional activities as a means of practicing specific structures, but everything we tried was somehow disappointing. These activities lacked spark, imagination, and, most of all, the students' voices. So next we tried journals, free-writing, and focused-topic writing. Students explored their own ideas in writing, but they tended to use the structures they were familiar with rather than the newly learned ones we wanted them to practice. Not satisfactory for our purposes! Finally, we tried a few well-known poems with simple patterns, such as haiku and cinquain, in the hope that students would be led to practice *specific* grammar points while becoming engaged with language and communication at a deeper, more personal level. With the very first poems our students wrote, we knew we were on to something special. Not only were our students practicing the structures we wanted them to, but they were also engaged and enthusiastic about the process. And the poems they wrote were little jewels!

In analyzing the success of the first poetic adventures with our students, we determined that what worked about the haiku and the cinquain was that both followed a very specific pattern, almost like a mold. Like a mold, each line of the pattern poems (as we later began to call them) had a preset form that allowed students to focus on pouring out their ideas rather than on worrying about the form those ideas would take. Having such a pattern predetermined for them was (perhaps paradoxically) liberating for our students, and they responded by writing creative pieces while practicing the specific structures inherent to each poem.

Along the way we discovered that pattern poems not only allowed for practicing grammatical structures but also turned out to be useful vehicles for a host of other purposes: vocabulary, spelling, pronunciation, speaking, listening, reading, language awareness, critical thinking, literary appreciation, and, obviously, writing. Although our initial motivation for using the poems had been grammar practice, the unintended benefits of writing pattern poems sometimes delightfully overshadowed our original purposes.

We shared our students' poems with anyone who would listen. We began compiling and self-publishing their pattern poetry and then circulated copies of the publications to other teachers and administrators. We gathered more poems, invented some, adapted others, and started presenting workshops to teachers from all levels – kindergarten to adult – teachers of native speakers and nonnative speakers alike. Those teachers were so impressed by the language learning and the quality of their students' pattern poems that they sent us copies to include in future workshops. They also invited us into their classrooms to share our lessons.

The result is the book of poetry lessons and poems you have in your hands. We have seen these poems work time and time again with both nonnative and native speakers, with students of all ages, and with students of varying levels of proficiency. We have seen students' language skills blossom along with their self-confidence as they produced poems that delighted and inspired us. We hope that you can use this book to help inspire the writing and language learning of your students, too.

Why write poems?

Hidden deep inside, each of us has a bit of the poet. Who among us cannot recite a short poem or nursery rhyme learned long ago? Or sing along with a tune on the radio even though we have not heard that song in years? Or recite our school song? Or sing a lullaby sung by our grandmother? Or recall an advertising jingle from years back?

How is it that many of us remember poetic language for years when we cannot remember the name of a person we met only minutes earlier? Poetry sticks with us because it resonates in our hearts and minds. The language of poetry grasps our imagination, emotions, and intellect with equal force regardless of our language backgrounds. Because poems often adhere to predictable patterns of rhythm and rhyme, they are pleasurable and easy to recall. Because they also easily tolerate unique word choice and phrasing, they help students overcome their sometimes paralyzing preoccupation with making mistakes. And because they are compact and economical in expression, they are a stimulating yet efficient medium for language learning. Although the poems in this book do not necessarily rhyme or have strict meter, their structure is often rhythmic, and they allow students to explore creative ways of communicating in writing without worrying about what form their ideas will take.

Poetry promotes language acquisition

Classroom teachers, teacher educators, and particularly parents know the value of using poetry to teach language skills. Children are often introduced to poetry early in their lives by parents, grandparents, and other caretakers who chant nursery rhymes or sing lullabies to soothe their children's anxiety – all before the youngsters have any consciousness of linguistic forms. Many children learn their first words from poems because the sounds of poetic language, with its patterns of rhythm, rhyme, and cadence, intrigue them and make them listen carefully. Linguists suggest that early knowledge of syntax comes from children listening to language forms from their environments. More often than not, those forms are poetic. Poetry teaches children to listen, develop vocabulary, learn to read and write, and think creatively. Poetry takes the structure and beauty of language and provides a personal world to explore.

For some of the same reasons that poetry is useful in acquisition of a first language, it is an effective way of learning and reinforcing the sounds and structures of a second, or even third, language. Through listening to poetry, second language learners can reinforce target language learning in a natural way. Added benefits accrue when second language students engage in poetry writing – especially pattern poem writing. The uses and benefits of writing pattern poems are greater than their apparent simplicity suggests. Through writing simple pattern poems, learners can:

- play with words and see what fits because the burden of discovering a proper format for a poem is removed
- create a polished piece of writing in a relatively short period, thereby experiencing "instant gratification"
- rehearse correct spelling
- use familiar vocabulary
- discover new vocabulary while using the dictionary or thesaurus to find words that serve their vision
- practice specific language structures such as phrases, word order, and verb tense
- develop confidence in their ability to share ideas in writing
- nurture creativity by giving their imaginations free reign
- cultivate logical and sequential thinking skills through storytelling
- refine summarizing skills

Despite their simple, uncomplicated nature, pattern poems reinforce, and even teach, multiple language skills while challenging students to share their vision of the world around them in a nonthreatening way. Most patterns can be used with all levels and ages of learners. Even those who are not yet literate in English can dictate poems for their teacher to write.

Using the book

Overview

Writing Simple Poems can be used in many ways. Although its specific purpose is for reinforcing language concepts, it can be used for encouraging creative writing, supporting literature, understanding content knowledge, building student confidence – or just for fun! No matter what your purpose, you can use the lessons side by side with your regular text to enrich instruction.

Writing Simple Poems is as easy to follow as a recipe book. And, as with a cookbook, each recipe (lesson) stands alone. This handbook can be opened to any lesson, where a complete, self-contained plan, set up in a predictable fashion following the same pattern, may be found. Thus, you will not need to invest a lot of time learning to use the book. Teach one chapter and you are a master chef! And, just as a master chef experiments with a recipe, we encourage you to spice up the activities and adapt them to your own uses.

To make the book user-friendly, we have set up each lesson with the following simple headings:

- *Teaching points.* These are points in language or writing that we believe can be taught through the pattern.
- *Pattern.* This is a line-by-line description of the form and content of the poem. To demonstrate the pattern, we include several models of the poem (which we wrote or adapted from student ideas) to give you a quick glimpse at what the poem might look like.
- *What to do.* This is a step-by-step process for introducing the poem and facilitating student writing. It can form the basis for a self-contained lesson plan.
- *Uses.* These are suggestions for integrating the poems into the overall curricula, linking them to content areas as well as language arts.
- *Variations.* These demonstrate modified forms of the poetic pattern, providing the bases for additional activities or lessons.
- *Student-written examples.* Examples of poems written by students of all ages and levels demonstrate the versatility of the patterns. Because the examples are authentic, they do not always follow the pattern *exactly,* thereby demonstrating the flexibility of the poetic forms and the creativity of the students and their teachers. These examples can be shared with your students to inspire their own creativity and to provide an enjoyable reading experience.

The teaching points in each chapter are cross-referenced in the *Index.* The *Glossary* provides explanations and examples of key language terms covered in the book.

Teaching pattern poems

We, the authors, have strong beliefs (even biases) on how to teach grammar and writing – on how to teach anything, for that matter. Our beliefs are demonstrated in the instructions of each lesson plan. They include:

- *Interactive modeling.* One of the assumptions of social learning theory is that students learn from observation and interaction with others in their immediate environment. With many poems, we suggest that the teacher write the poem *with* the class so that students can participate in the process with a guide (interactive modeling). By thinking aloud with the students while writing their words on the board, teachers can demonstrate how writers decide what to write about, which words to use, where to place words on the page, and when revision is needed. For example, the teacher might say, "Let's see. You suggested writing: 'I like to swim.' But we have already used the word *like*. What other words could we use?" Students might volunteer the words *enjoy, love,* or *adore*. Through negotiation, the students decide on the best word to use. Students easily learn writing strategies from writing *with* the teacher, a learning process that then supports them in writing their own poems.
- *Collaborative groups.* Groups collaborate when they work on the *same* piece of writing together. Interactive modeling is one form of collaborative learning because the students have helped the teacher create the same poem as a whole group process. The logical extension is to use small groups of students as collaborative learning units for writing poems. Students become responsible for creating a single poem or part of a poem as a group rather than as individuals. They learn from and with each other as they negotiate the meanings of words, select which words to use, and construct phrasing. Pressure to perform, often resulting in writer's block, is minimized as the responsibility for writing is shared. The resulting poem becomes a tribute to the group's creativity and language control, bringing satisfaction and unity to the group.
- *Cooperative groups.* Cooperative group work involves students helping each other with *individually written* pieces. While students are writing their own individual poems, they can cooperate with others in their group by brainstorming for ideas and words, structuring their poems, or responding to each others' drafts. Peer response, through cooperative groups, reinforces the connection between readers and writers. It increases the flow of language and builds fluency.
- *Inductive thinking.* Most of the poems in this book have distinct structural patterns that can be shown and explained to students before they start writing. An alternative to this kind of deductive approach is

to encourage students to figure out the patterns themselves. Showing students models and asking them to find the pattern is a wonderful exercise in inductive reasoning. Some of the patterns, such as the cinquain (Lesson 10), lend themselves particularly well to this approach. The ability to infer or discover structure in a grouping of words encourages hypothesis testing, which is essential for critical reasoning as well as language acquisition. We advocate using an inductive approach when the material allows. Discovering the patterns themselves, rather than having the teacher point them out, gives students a feeling of ownership and control over the poems.

- *Sensory stimulation.* Whenever possible, we have suggested that you use sensory stimuli (especially visual) to spur the creative process and give students something concrete to write about. For example, students find it much easier to write a haiku (Lesson 17) when they have a colorful picture of a nature scene to stimulate them. By the same token, students can discover and describe the differences between two items when writing the contrast poem (Lesson 12) if they have two contrasting items to study visually. Video clips also stimulate the production of words and concepts and make an exciting introduction to poetry writing. Music selections, textures that students feel, foods to taste, and other sensory stimuli can be incorporated into the poetry lessons to enhance the creative process.

- *Sharing students' poems.* We strongly believe in sharing students' writing within the classroom, in the school community, and beyond. There are so many ways to share students' work that entire books have been written on the topic. Some ways that we have experienced include:

  - big book anthologies made up of individual or class-written poems that can be used for reading activities in other students' classes
  - individual poetry readings in both private (e.g., classroom) and public (e.g., auditorium) forums
  - choral readings performed in class or for other classes
  - tapes of poetry readings for building oral skills
  - simple publications of both individual and group poems run off on the copy machine and distributed to family members, the school community, the local library, and so on
  - poetry greeting cards, calendars, recipe books, and so on
  - poetry tag, a game in which students carry poems they wrote in their pockets and can be "tagged" (chosen) to read their poems by another writer

For us, the principal reasons for sharing student poems in the classroom are the following:

- The poems turn out to be more interesting because students have a chance to hear and look at one another's ideas and writing styles.
- Students get to practice oral language as they help each other search for words and edit their poems during the writing process. They also practice oral language as they read their poems aloud for their groups and for the class at the end of an activity.
- Students learn from each other and about each other by writing for an audience other than the teacher. Not only do they learn language from each other as they swap words and ideas or negotiate the meaning of a phrase, but they also learn what other students think is important or meaningful.
- Students develop confidence in their ability to communicate in the target language. Seeing their poems posted on the bulletin board or printed on the page of a poetry publication becomes visual testimony to their evolving fluency. Hearing their poems read aloud in choral readings or reading them aloud themselves to an audience of fellow poets provides proof of students' communication skills.
- Students develop an appreciation and respect for one another as they compose side by side and together. Engaged in the same activity with the same associated risks, they become a community of writers with a shared identity. This feeling builds cohesion in the class, which carries over to other activities.
- Most students *enjoy* reading other students' poems and having their own poems read.

Sharing student poetry with a wider audience such as the school community, parents, relatives, friends, neighbors, and the community at large is very appealing for other reasons:

- Displays, publications, and performance of student poems give parents and teachers an opportunity to celebrate student success, and it makes all parties involved proud.
- Positive attention is focused on the students, a teacher, and/or the school involved in a poetry project that is shared publicly. This attention can be used pragmatically to attract needed resources to support other programs or simply be a point of pride. One elementary school in our district with mostly second language learners has chosen to become a "poetry school." Teachers regularly engage students in poetry writing, posting their poems on bulletin boards, in newsletters, and in the library. Being a poetry school has given this school a unique and positive identity, a source of pride for everyone in the school.

- *Linking poetry to content.* One powerful aspect of poetry writing is that it can – and should – be linked to content that students are learning in their classes. Language does not operate in a vacuum. We use the language we acquire to communicate about the world we live in and about the things we are discovering. Many teachers have used pattern poems to reinforce concepts learned in mathematics, social sciences, hard sciences, history, and the like. Some have used the poems as a form of report or summary of short stories or books that students have read. We provide multiple examples of how poetry can be used in the various disciplines to reinforce not only language and structure, but also content. See, for example, Lessons 1, 7, and 22.

- *Celebrating diversity.* In multilingual classes, students enjoy sharing their languages and cultures with other learners. Many of the poems in this book lend themselves to cultural topics such as holidays, foods, historical events, and famous people. Even specific words from students' native languages can be incorporated in poems to add authenticity and diversity. Some poems can take on a bilingual, bicultural flavor when they use two languages (see student poems in Lessons 1 and 14). We encourage you to let your students – especially those at the early stages of fluency – experiment with their native language and English together. The results are often stunning.

Keep in mind

Age versus language proficiency. English-proficiency level and age are not always directly related. As you read the student-written poems, you will notice that some of the more "sophisticated" poems are written by younger learners, whereas some of the "simple" poems are written by adult learners. This demonstrates that English proficiency arrives at all stages of life and that these poems lend themselves to student use during all phases of learning. Adult learners are not put off by simple poems if they are appropriate to their level of English acquisition.

Cultural connections. Poetry and culture are intimately entwined, so you will notice that the poems in this book are very American; the poems' subjects (holidays, brand names, and sight-seeing attractions), as well as some of the terms we have used (*scratch paper* and *cooperative learning,* for example), may seem like "Americanisms." That is because we *are* Americans, and the students we worked with were learning English in the United States. If you live elsewhere, we hope you will substitute examples and terms more appropriate for *your* students and the countries in which you live and teach English. This should not be an issue, for students are eager to write about what is familiar to them.

Editing student writing. Deciding how much to edit student writing when that writing will be published is a thorny issue. We were torn between feelings of wanting to maintain the authenticity of the students' voices while not wanting to embarrass student writers by publishing multiple mistakes. We resolved the problem by asking students to edit their work as much as they could. We then corrected spelling, word-form errors, and minor grammatical mistakes such as subject-verb agreement. We did not correct word order, word choice, or any "mistake" that would alter the students' creations.

Origins. Some of the patterns presented in this book may be familiar. Like your grandmother's favorite recipe, they have been passed from one person to the next, adapted and changed over time. Because they are hand-me-down poems, it is impossible to acknowledge their origins, but, as you use them, we hope you'll add your own seasonings to suit your and your students' tastes.

Alphabetical organization. Originally we arranged the lessons according to our perceptions of the difficulty of the poems, starting with the "simple" poems. As we taught the lessons to students of varying ages, language backgrounds, and English proficiency, we soon learned that this sort of organization was unrealistic. We saw that *any* of the poems could be made simple or complex depending on how they were introduced and on the language level of the student involved. It occurred to us that the only nonprejudicial way to organize was alphabetically. Therefore, we recommend that you not attempt to start at the beginning with "A" and work your way through the book. Better to use the Index to find the language point or topic you want to reinforce with your students and go from there!

Poetry is infectious. Once you use several of these poems, we predict that both you and your students will be hooked. We also predict that when other teachers hear about your students' success, they will want to join in. Through working with our own adult students, as well as with younger learners in other classrooms, we discovered that poetry writing is infectious and habit-forming. Because the process is so enjoyable, students look forward to poetry-writing sessions. And because the poems are so original and inspiring, teachers and students want to share their work in a public forum. Soon the word gets around and everyone wants a copy of the "recipe." Like a good recipe, the student-written poems these patterns inspire are meant to be shared and savored. We urge you to encourage the poetry habit and to get other teachers in on the act.

Practical tips

We have actually used the lessons in this book with students of different ages and English-language levels. Using the trial-and-error method, we learned from the students what worked and what didn't. We also learned from the other teachers who worked with us. We revised the lessons and taught them again with other teachers and to other students until we got them right. During the process, we made some observations that you might find useful:

Timing. We had lots of issues regarding timing:

- when to introduce the poems
- how often to use them
- how much time to allow to complete a lesson
- how much time to allow for revision
- how much time to set aside for sharing

We were able to resolve all of our timing issues, but not without some false starts. First, we learned that the poems work best when they are introduced *after* students have studied a language point through direct instruction. We had our best results when students already understood the parts of speech or phrasing of a given poem and merely used the poem to practice language. We did use some poems with groups for the purpose of teaching a language concept for the first time. The results were mixed, so we recommend that you use the poems for reinforcement rather than for introducing language points.

Second, using the poems too frequently (i.e., too many days in a row) is not a good idea, from the perspective either of language acquisition or of lesson planning. Students need to have time to digest what they have learned from writing the poems, make revisions to their work, and practice language in other ways as well. We recommend that you use the poems to *punctuate* your lessons – sort of as a reward to students for learning a new concept – rather than in a habitual, predictable way.

No matter how simple the poem, we discovered that it takes about one class period (50 minutes) to introduce and complete a poetry lesson. That does not count time for revising and editing, which we believe to be an essential and rewarding step for the students. On several occasions, we had planned to teach two very simple (or so we thought!) poems to a group of fairly fluent students. It did not work because the students merely took the poem to another level *because of* their fluency and it still took a class period to finish one poem. We recommend that you allow at least one class period for each poem. Don't rush the process.

How much time you allow for revision will depend on a number of factors, not the least of which is the level of proficiency of your students. We found that revision generally takes less time for beginners than it does for advanced students, even though the beginners might have more "errors" to address. Beginners often do not have the language skills to recognize their own errors, nor do they have the vocabulary to make many changes in content. Advanced students often take longer. No matter what level you are teaching, we suggest that you *do* leave time to help students "clean up" their poems. We believe that students prefer to have good, sound writing they can proudly share with others, and that they are willing to take the time to revise if there is a clear purpose.

We suggest you make time for students to share their poems *soon* after they have written them – preferably the same day. The time needed for sharing will depend on the size and fluency of your class, the length and complexity of the poem, and the number of poems written (e.g., twenty individual poems or five group poems). These points need to be considered so that you don't run out of time, leaving one or two students' or groups' poems unread. When this happened to us, it had a discouraging effect on the students. Consequently, we made sure to plan sufficient time for sharing, which could vary from 5 to 15 minutes for oral readings.

Supporting writing. How much support students need while writing the poems depends on their level of English proficiency as well as their resourcefulness and motivation. How much support you *choose* to give them, however, depends on your philosophy as a teacher and how you answer these questions:

- Should I suggest vocabulary?
- Should I offer ideas to write about?
- Should I help with spelling?
- Which materials should I have in the classroom?
- How can I help reluctant writers?

Because there are no right answers to these questions, we can only share what we did and what we observed other teachers do in the way of supporting their students' writing.

Like most of the teachers we observed, we tried to coax as much out of the students as possible by giving hints, clues, and resources that would help them with word selection, idea generation, or just getting started. Most teachers, like us, tried to avoid handing students the "answers." For instance, when the third-grade students wanted help with brainstorming adverbs for the "Adverb poem" (Lesson 4), the teacher told them to think of at least one adverb on their own and then use a thesaurus for ideas for more adverbs. Her suggestion was very effective because she had the resources available in her classroom. Another teacher had students create word banks (of adjectives, for example) that covered the whole board so students could select from among those generated by the group rather than depend on themselves alone for all the vocabulary. But if students just didn't have a word at their command to express a concept they wanted in their poem, we, like other teachers, weren't averse to using that opportunity to teach a new word. A perfect teaching moment!

We used that same philosophy when it came to idea generation. We learned that some students get "stuck" trying to decide *what* to write about, and they waste a lot of time just getting started. To avoid wasted energy, we had the class generate lists of ideas to write about before turning the students loose to write on their own or in small groups. We covered the board with those ideas or wrote them on small slips of paper that could be drawn from a hat. In the case of students who had ideas but seemed afraid to write them down, we helped them get started by taking dictation from them. Other times we provided them with handouts on which the first words of the poem were already written. Just having something on their paper seemed to loosen up the reluctant writers enough to begin writing their own ideas.

With regard to spelling, few teachers sent their students to dictionaries. Most spelled the word for the students or, better yet, told them to do their best and worry about spelling later. Like us, they believed that if the students are in the process of writing, then stopping to look up words interferes with their train of thought. We recommend that you teach your students that correcting spelling is part of the editing process. Initially, getting ideas on the paper is more important. They can correct spelling later.

Having a class set of dictionaries and thesauruses on hand is very helpful for error correction or for brainstorming vocabulary. Unfortunately, many of the classes we taught in had neither, so we toted along sets for students to share. We didn't need one for each student, just one for each group. We found that students enjoyed leafing through the pages looking for just the right word. If your school cannot provide these resources, you might find yourself acting as the word genie because, once students get involved in poetry writing, they realize the importance of having that one "right" word!

As to helping reluctant writers, we have found that some of the same devices that help *all* writers seem to be almost *essential* for those who have a hard time getting started: for example, word banks written on the board, topic starters written on slips of paper or note cards, video clips taken from action movies, or colorful pictures torn from magazines. For especially hesitant writers, however, we like to use pair work. We have observed that pairing hesitant with eager writers and having them write *one* poem together allows the enthusiasm and confidence of the eager writer to "rub off" on the reluctant one. Over time, reluctant writers often develop a sense of confidence as they see their poems – even though written with a partner – in print and hear them read aloud. They can then be freed from the support they derive from working with a confident writer to work on their own!

Sharing. As we've already said, we believe that sharing is essential. We observed several different methods for sharing the first day's efforts at writing a poem. The third-grade teacher had everyone sit in a circle on the floor to indicate that it was sharing time. She began each sharing time with a poem she had written during the same time period, reading it loudly and slowly to model good oral reading. The fourth-grade teacher had each student stand and face the class to read aloud to make sure everyone could hear. Middle-school, high-school, and adult teachers had their students do the same.

Students at lower levels of language proficiency seemed to share their poetry better when we had them rewrite their finished draft on a transparency so that the other students could *see* the words at the same time that they heard them. Students' being able to see and hear at the same time nullifies some of the pronunciation errors and inaudible voices that interfere with oral comprehension. With pairs or small groups, the writers often performed choral readings to take away the pressure of having to read alone in front of their peers. Poems written by the whole class were always reread aloud as a group. The important point is the visual aid. We recommend that you use some form of visual aid, be it transparencies, board, or flip charts, to assist students with their oral presentations.

In every case, the students applauded each other's work after hearing it read. They basked in the praise the applause signaled. We recommend that you lead the applause if the students don't start it spontaneously.

As well as being shared orally, the poems in every case were also published in various ways. With word-processing programs that make font size and formatting easy to control, these publications took various forms. The youngest students enjoyed having their own poems printed in large type on a single sheet that they could illustrate and "frame" on construction paper. After displaying their illustrated poems for a while, some teachers laminated each one and bound them all together in a "big book" for students to look at later. Other teachers created anthologies. One teacher saved her students' work and created individual books of all the poems that each student had written. Other teachers created anthologies of all the students' poems together. These anthologies used a colorful cover sheet and were bound with plastic spirals. No matter the age, students autographed one another's books and, again, basked in the praise they received from other students, their teachers, and their relatives. The books were easy and inexpensive to create and, based on the students' expressions of delight, well worth the time and effort.

Enjoyment. Don't underestimate the value of the poetry writing for the sheer joy that it brings the students. Our students often cheer when we announce that it is time to write poetry. Perhaps that is because writing pattern poems offers a nice break from normal routine while providing plenty of opportunity for language work and self-expression. Perhaps it is because students enjoy the chance to be involved in an activity that doesn't seem like "work." Or perhaps they enjoy the writing because it results in the creation of a visible mini-monument that they can point to and say, "I did that!"

1 Acrostic

Teaching points: Spelling
Vocabulary
Dictionary usage

The acrostic can be a simple poem to write, but it can be made more challenging. Spelling is emphasized for the key word of the acrostic, but use of the dictionary can also be taught to enrich vocabulary.

Furry face	**F**unny	**F**ew people are
Red hair	**R**eal	**R**eal friends
Intelligent eyes	**I**nteresting	**I**n my life. I
Ears that hear everything	**E**njoyable	**E**njoy seeing true, not
Nose that sniffs	**N**ice	**N**ew friends every
Dog of my dreams	**D**elightful	**D**ay

Pattern

Select a word or name and write it in a column on the left side of the paper (as has been done with "word" below).

W (select a word, phrase, or sentence beginning with the letter of the word being spelled down the left column)

O (select a word, phrase, or sentence beginning with the second letter of the word in the left column)

R (select a word, phrase, or sentence beginning with the third letter

D (select a word, phrase, or sentence beginning with the fourth letter)

Continue the pattern for each letter in the word.

What to do

1. Explain what an acrostic is, that it spells out a word in a column and then explains the word in words or phrases beginning with each letter of the word. Show the students some samples and ask then to identify the word each one is about by having them read the first letter of each line.
2. Select a word or name that is an example of the acrostic students will be writing: your name, a place-name, a character's name, a book title, an animal, a science or math concept, or any noun about which the students have knowledge. For a short poem, for instance, you might select the word *school,* whereas for a longer example you might select the proper name of your school. Using capital letters, write the word on the chalkboard in a column:

S
C
H
O
O
L

3. Explain to the students that you are going to write a poem made up of words (or phrases or sentences, depending on the level of students) that begin with these letters and that express your knowledge and attitude toward it. If, for instance, you selected the word *school,* you might then say, "I know that 'students' and 'studying' are part of school. I think I like 'students' better, so I'll use that." Using the *s* in the column that spells *school,* write the word *students:*

Students

Make sure the first letter is larger and bolder than the rest so that it is obvious you are spelling the word in the left column.

4. Continue with the next letter of the word, asking students for suggestions of words. Continue until all the letters have a word, phrase, or sentence attached. A very simple poem on school might turn out to be something like this:

Student
Community
Helpfully
Offering
Opportunities
Learning

A more sophisticated poem might wrap from one line to the next to form a single sentence, as in the following:

Students learn from teachers
Cool stuff that will
Help them earn credits in
Order to go to college and have
Opportunities to better their
Lives.
– Joannie Monroy's class (ages 15 to 17)

5. Read the entire poem aloud. Ask students if they can think of anything they want to change or add. In the simpler poem above, you might suggest adding the word *for* to the fifth line:

Student
Community
Helpfully
Offering
Opportunities for
Learning

Making such a change allows you to point out not only the need for revision, but also the freedom this poem allows.

6. Your students should now be ready to practice writing their own acrostics individually, in pairs, or in small groups. This is a good opportunity to encourage them to browse through dictionaries or the glossaries of their course books for words that start with a particular letter.

Uses

- to introduce each student and his or her name
- to explore attitudes and emotions toward an idea
- to define or describe an animal, a geographic location, an abstract concept, or some other content-related idea
- to explain a concept in the student's native language that may defy direct translation but could be described
- to summarize the plot or describe a character in a book the student has read

Variations

- To teach dictionary and spelling skills, you can select words that students know but have difficulty spelling. For instance, many students misspell *friend, which, responsible,* and *grammar.* Have students use a word that has been marked as a spelling error on a paper and look it up in the dictionary, copy the correct spelling, and then write an acrostic of the word to focus students on the word's spelling in connection with its meaning.

- To teach specific types of phrases, require that students use only the type you have selected. Noun phrases (e.g., "big black cat") and verb phrases (e.g., "hurrying to the classroom") work especially well with the acrostic.

Student-written examples

Dinosaurs
Iguanodon
Nodosaurus
Oviraptor
Stegosaurus
Allosaurus
Ultrasaurus
Raptor
—Elizabeth Gordon
    Taylor's class
    (ages 6 to 7)

About 13 feet long
Live a long time
Like to eat a variety of food
Insects and tadpoles make a meal for babies
Grow to weigh up to 500 pounds
Adults eat fish and small mammals
The babies grow 12 inches a year
Once widely hunted for their skin
Related to the Chinese alligator
—Jasmine Espinoza, Andrea Cabrera,
    Antonio Arias, Jose Ramirez, Leslie
    Ramirez, Davis Martinez
    (ages 8 and 9)

Grape lover
Always looks in the mirror
Bossy (Hey!)
Redheaded
Intelligent (5 × 5 = 25)
Excellent student (Yes!)
Likes the library
Loves money ($$$)
Extra nice
—Gabrielle McAdory (age 9)

Many kinds of methods to use in
Almost everything you do.
Thinking is required, and so are
Hundreds of terms and numbers.
—Davin Tso (age 12)

Music loving
Lucky
Athletic
Delightful
Excellent
Never gives up
Kitten loving
Able
—Mladenka Antunovic
  (age 13)

She was a beautiful, lonely girl.
No one could see how beautiful she was.
Only the seven dwarves knew
Where she lived.
Why were
Her friends taking care of her
In the little house in the forest?
The witch was trying to
End her life.
—Karla Chacon (age 15), Joel Bejarano
  (age 16), Moses Araujo (age 17)

Students from all around the United States
Prepare to have fun vacations
Rolling with their friends
In all kinds of places.
Nobody stays at home.
Girls and boys flock to the
Beach to forget school and
Relax in the nice hot sun.
Everybody wants to stay
And they all want to
Kick back with their friends forever. .
—Francisco Tlatelpa (age 14), Rafael Peña (age 16),
  Cesar Gonzalez (age 16)

True story of love and
Interesting characters
Triangle between two men
And a woman stuck on a ship with
No way to escape
Iceberg
Crashed into the ship and sank the lovers
—Sneha Patel (age 16), Javier Camarena (age 15),
  Ricardo Bermudez (age 16)

Missing you so much
In my heart
Now that I don't have you next to me
Anymore.
My heart will
Always be yours forever.
How can I forget your
Angel-like face and
Loving soul?
—PeeJay Tagudin (age 16), Ivis Cruz-Antuñez (age 15),
   Melisa Cejas (age 14) (*Minamahal* is a Philippine
   word meaning "I'm missing you")

Valentine's Day is
A special day for all
Lovers and friends.
Every Valentine's Day
Nothing is better than to receive and
To give a big smile, a hug, or a kiss.
In every heart there is a feeling,
Not a bad one but the sweetest one.
Everyone likes to enjoy this day with his
Sweetheart,
Day and night,
All the days of the
Year.
—Bertha Hernandez (age 15), Elizabeth Caro (age 15),
   Leonardo Cejas (age 14)

Chill out, honorable mates! Calm down.
Leave no more to the insecure.
Aim so well to a free ground, and
Seek your future. Don't lose your cool.
Strong and free you have to be.
Modify your path, look for your throne,
Apply your efforts, use your skills.
Triumph is your target. Triumph is your goal.
Elevate your spirit. Clean up your soul.
Strong and free you have to be.
—Apolo Acosta (adult)

2 Adjective poem

Teaching points: Adjectives
Adjectives after linking verbs
Thesaurus usage

The adjective poem consists of six lines developing a series of adjectives to describe a single topic or action. It can provide good practice for merely identifying and creating adjectives without needing to worry about the appropriate order, which is addressed in Lesson 3 ("Adjective placement poem").

Ricky Martin

Ricky Martin is handsome

Ricky Martin is handsome, sexy

Is handsome, sexy, popular

Handsome, sexy, popular, Latino

Singer

Babies

Babies are cute

Babies are cute, cuddly

Are cute, cuddly, curious

Cute, cuddly, curious, noisy

Children

Pattern

Line 1: Noun
Line 2: Same noun + is or are + adjective 1
Line 3: Same noun + is or are + adjective 1, adjective 2
Line 4: Is or are + adjective 1, adjective 2, adjective 3
Line 5: Adjective 1, adjective 2, adjective 3,
        adjective 4
Line 6: New related noun

What to do

1. Tell students that they are going to create a poem using mainly adjectives. To check their understanding of adjectives, list some nouns and ask them to provide adjectives for them. Some possible nouns include *dog, rain,* and *friend.* Students should be able to name several adjectives for each noun.

2. Ask students where adjectives are placed when describing a person, place, or thing. Most students will probably know that adjectives are placed before a noun in English, but they may not recognize that adjectives may also be placed after a linking verb such as *to be*.

3. Show examples of sentences with adjectives before the noun and after a linking verb:

The pretty girl smiled at me.   Maria is pretty.
The baby made funny sounds.   The baby's sounds were funny.

4. Have them identify the parts of speech in the second set of sentences and explain that the poem they will be writing will place the adjectives after a linking verb as these sentences do.

5. Show students several samples of the adjective poem and ask them to identify the parts of speech in each line. Because the adjectives are repeated, have them number the adjectives to identify the pattern of repetition:

Noun
Fog
Noun   verb   adjective 1
Fog is white
Noun   verb   adjective 1   adjective 2
Fog is white, wet
Verb   adjective 1   adjective 2   adjective 3
Is white, wet, thick
Adjective 1   adjective 2   adjective 3   adjective 4
White, wet, thick, cold
Noun
Morning

6. Ask the students for a topic on which they can write a poem together. Select one and ask the students to brainstorm adjectives that describe the topic.

7. Have the students select four of the adjectives they generated to describe the topic. Number the adjectives 1, 2, 3, and 4, and then have the students tell you where to place the adjectives in each line.

8. Ask for a synonym or closely associated words to use as the final line. Select one to finish the poem.

9. Divide students into small groups to write their own poems. Have cards prepared with topics listed on them in case your students have difficulty thinking of their own topics. Some topics we have used include:

Halloween	Mickey Mouse	Bubble gum
Christmas	Donald Duck	Sweaters
Horses	McDonald's	Summer
Kittens	Disneyland	Noses
The students' school	Tacos	Jeep
Santa Claus	Chocolate ice cream	Sports cars
Winter	Lemons	

If students have a difficult time thinking of adjectives, encourage them to look up the definition of their noun in the dictionary to see if it gives them ideas for adjectives. Once they think of one adjective, they can also use a thesaurus to find other words related to that adjective.

10. Have students read aloud the completed poems to their classmates.
11. Your students should now be ready to write their own individual adjective poems.

Uses

- to describe a topic within a subject area (weather phenomena, animals, mathematical concepts)
- to describe a person or character

Student-written examples

Snow people
Snow people are icy
Snow people are icy, soft
Are icy, soft, fun
Icy, soft, fun, frozen
Snow men and ladies
—Angela Miller (age 6)

Twisters
Twisters are gray
Twisters are gray, spinning
Are gray, spinning, dusty
Gray, spinning, dusty, scary
Tornados
—Celeste Romero-Garcia (age 7)

Crayfish
Crayfish are quick
Crayfish are quick, mysterious
Are quick, mysterious, red
Quick, mysterious, red, small
Crustaceans
—Rudy Rodriguez (age 9)

Pollution
Pollution is contaminated
Pollution is contaminated, foul
Is contaminated, foul, tainted
Contaminated, foul, tainted, dirty
Poison
—Ileana Gonzalez (age 9)

Halloween
Halloween is scary
Halloween is scary, fun
Is scary, fun, tasty
Scary, fun, tasty, dangerous
Night
—Jessica Andrade (age 12),
   Leslie Marquez (age 12),
   Martha Reza (age 13),
   Aileen Ruiz (age 13)

Noses
Noses are straight
Noses are straight, ugly
Are straight, ugly, big
Straight, ugly, big, smelly
Nariz
—Ler Say Htay (age 12),
   Ler Law Lah Htay (age 13),
   Lay Mu Khu Htay (age 11)

Guacamole
Guacamole is delicious
Guacamole is delicious, spicy
Is delicious, spicy, smooth
Delicious, spicy, smooth, creamy
Snack
—Eduardo Campos (age 16),
   Juan Jurado (age 16)

Santa Claus
Santa Claus is old
Santa Claus is old, bearded
Is old, bearded, jolly
Old, bearded, jolly, fat
Father Christmas
—Jim Gacula (age 18),
   Mariano Alba (age 15)

Bubble gum
Bubble gum is soft
Bubble gum is soft, sweet
Is soft, sweet, swell
Soft, sweet, swell, exploding
Dream
—Hyesook Moon (adult)

Piano
Piano is black
Piano is black, white
Is black, white, perfect
Black, white, perfect, touchable
Sound
—Unyoung Son (adult)

3 Adjective placement poem

Teaching points: Adjectives
Order of adjectives in a noun phrase
Vocabulary

Because the order of adjectives in sentences varies among languages, English-language students must often be directly taught the preferred order of elements (especially adjectives) in a noun phrase. Such order has been amply analyzed through the use of transcribed speech and written texts. The results show that a relatively fixed ordering exists, though it is occasionally violated by native speakers. In their advanced texts, most grammarians include charts or lists of the order of adjectives – see, for example, Chapter 28 in M. Celce-Murcia, and D. Larsen-Freeman, *The Grammar Book,* Rowley, Mass., Newbury House (1983). The following chart contains a list of attributive adjectives based on such texts, which you may want to simplify for your students.

Order of adjectives

1. determiners	5. general description	9. color
2. possessive words	6. size, height, length	10. origin
3. ordinal numbers	7. shape	11. nouns as adjectives
4. cardinal numbers	8. age, temperature	12. head noun

1   5   6   8   9   10   11   12
a beautiful big old brown Italian leather sofa

2   3   4   5   8   11   12
our first three pleasant warm winter days

1   5   7   9   10   11   12
a valuable oval gold French picture frame

Although no more than three adjectives are generally used in sequence in both oral and written English, knowing the proper sequence can be very useful. Students are often taught this sequencing with the use of charts and fill-in-the-blank written and oral activities. One variation of this type of traditional instruction is to have students write adjective placement poems.

I'm taking a trip to Disneyland
I'm taking along all of my favorite things:
A big, old leather scrapbook
My four, black Mickey Mouse dolls
A blue, striped, bikini bathing suit
Some yellow rubber ducks for my bath
And, of course, my silly little baby sister

My first three sets of playing cards
A powerful GE hairdryer
All my precious, shiny Tom Cruise pictures
My fluffy white feather pillow
And many happy memories to bring me back home.

Pattern

Choose a destination. You won't be returning for a very long time, so think of special things you'll need to keep you happy, favorite things that you can't bear to be without for a long time.

Line 1   I'm (we're) taking a trip to _____
Line 2   And I'm (we're) taking all of my (our) favorite things:
Line 3 ⎫
Line 4 ⎪
Line 5 ⎬ Noun clauses with descriptive adjectives
Line 6 ⎪
Line 7 ⎭ (last line begins with "and")

The five-line stanza above can be repeated with new noun phrases as long as the students have items they wish to describe. One option is to give the poem closure by having the last line refer to returning from the vacation.

What to do

1. Before introducing the poem, you may want to review the order of adjectives using the chart at the beginning of this lesson. One activity that helps check students' understanding involves sets of cards consisting of a number of adjectives and one noun, all of which the

students must place in the proper order. Using Set 1, a student pair or group might receive a set of cards in the following order:

| round | dish | candy | crystal | the | short |

The students must rearrange the cards as follows:

| the | short | round | crystal | candy | dish |

Some sets that we have used are the following:

Set 1	Set 2	Set 3
the	the	a
short	first	lovely
round	exciting	little
crystal	Warrior	ten-year-old
candy	basketball	girl
dish	game	

Set 4	Set 5	Set 6
some	a	my
delicious	stylish	old
hot	new	fat
pepperoni	red	black
pizza	dress	dog

Set 7	Set 8	Set 9
the	some	three
long	valuable	handsome
cold	old	brown-eyed
gray	German	Mexican
winter	stamps	boys
months		

2. Show your students several examples of the poem to stimulate their creativity. Ask them to notice the pattern by comparing at least two examples. They should notice that the only thing that changes in the first two lines is the destination. They should also notice that the rest of the lines (except, perhaps, for the last line) consist of noun phrases with several adjectives modifying each noun. The last line can be either the final item or a means of summing up the poem.

3. Ask students to think of places (real or imaginary) as destinations. Write them on the board. After generating a list of six or seven, ask students to pick the destination that is the most exciting. Write that destination in large letters in the center of the board preceded by these words: "We're taking a trip to . . ." Underneath the first line, write: "We're taking all of our favorite things:"

   If you want to make this an activity that reinforces student knowledge of vocabulary related to life in particular geographic locations, you may want to change the second line to "We're taking some things to help us survive."

4. Form groups of two or three students per group. Explain that each group will be responsible for deciding on an indispensable item or items to take on the trip. Tell them that there is no limit to what they can take and that it doesn't have to be "logical." Instruct them to use lots of descriptive words to help the reader understand *exactly* what their item is.

5. While students are writing their lines, distribute markers and large, precut slips of paper (about 20 inches by 4 inches) onto which they can transpose their lines. You may also want to check for proper placement of adjectives in their lines.

6. After all the groups have edited their lines and are satisfied with their creations, ask them to use markers to write their lines on the slips of paper.

7. Now, have one member from each group come forward to stick his or her slip of paper on the board following the previous lines. Students may want to rearrange the lines to achieve a more pleasing balance after they have had a chance to read the group poem.

8. Once students have experienced ordering adjectives in noun clauses, ask them to write a complete poem in each group. If students have difficulty thinking of destinations, you may want to assign them places such as a specific foreign country, an amusement park or recreation area, a relative's house, a restaurant, or other specific places such as a summer camp, jail, or shopping mall.

9. Completed poems can be exchanged with other groups to check adjective order. We have found it useful to have students use the charts to check their adjective order, numbering the adjectives with the categories they represent in the chart.

10. Have each group share its poem with the class by presenting it on an overhead transparency or reading it aloud.

Uses

- to describe events in the students' lives
- to introduce or reinforce vocabulary related to cultural and geographic sites

Student-written examples

A trip to Egypt
We're taking a trip to Egypt,
And we're taking along our favorite things:
My fun, rectangular, old, blue, Japanese Gameboy,
My big, sharp-beaked, old, singing, white and yellow cockatoo,
My soft, playful, short, small-eared, female black lab,
And we'll have fun!
—Gabrielle McAdory (age 9), Andy Romero (age 9),
   Carlos Piza (age 9)

Hawaii
We're taking a trip to Hawaii,
And we're taking along some of our favorite things:
Fifteen cool pop, rock, and rap CDs,
Three beautiful young girls to play with us on the beach,
Our three loony best friends,
Our white crystal soccer ball,
Our nineteen funny family members,
Our beautiful, good 35-year-old mother,
Thirty-five colored rectangular 'N Sync pictures
And $800 to buy all the crunchy Dorito chips, icy cold Coca Cola, and
   big green-leafed lettuce that we need so we never have to come
   back.
—Lance Egan's class (ages 11 to 13)

Lesson 3

Jail
We're taking a trip to jail,
And we're taking along our favorite things:
A big screen TV,
A huge JVC or Boss stereo,
Some metal safety underwear,
A comfy king-size water bed,
An extra pack of playing cards,
A warm, whirling jacuzzi,
And, most important, a successful lawyer to get us out.
—Francisco Tlatelpa (age 14), Rafael Pena (age 16),
  Cesar Gonzalez (age 16)

Brazil
In the summer, we will take a trip to Brazil.
We want to take some personal things:
A camera to take pictures of all the lovely bikini-clad ladies,
My blue swimming trunks,
My greasy sunblock to protect my skin from frying,
$13,000 dollars to spend in the nightclubs,
We will stay at a beautiful motel with an awesome view of the beach,
And in the morning we will go and see the Amazon River.
With all these things, we will have a wonderful trip in Brazil.
—Moses Araujo (age 16), Karla Chacon (age 15),
  Joel Bejarano (age 16)

The North Pole
We are taking a trip to the North Pole,
And we are taking along some necessary things:
A cup of delicious hot Colombian coffee,
A pair of nice, dark Oakley sunglasses,
A big, warm Nike hat,
And an expensive Hilfilger jacket.
Some nicely fitted snow boots,
A lot of low-fat healthy sweet foods,
A useful fishing kit to catch our dinner,
A bag of Snickers chocolate bars,
And last, a bottle of Mexican tequila.
—Taka Sugiyama, Juan Castillo, Ismenia Varela,
  San-Eun Lee (adults)

A trip to Hawaii

We are taking a trip to heaven on earth, Hawaii,

And we're taking our cherished possessions:

Angelica's expensive, very useful, small, electronic dictionary because
we want to keep communications with every hunk on the beach;

Bing's friendly, funny, intelligent twin brother to laugh and cry with, hit
the town with, and meet some gorgeous Hawaiian girls;

Min's amazing, valuable, great music CD collection to listen to while
we relax our bodies and minds with the Hawaiian people and
classmates;

Emi's cute, fantastic, small Jim Carrey photos since his smile is to die
for;

Noemi's handsome, tall, blond-haired, blue-eyed, lovely boyfriend so
she won't be alone in paradise;

Ana's favorite, interesting, incredibly funny book *Doctor* by E. Segal
just in case she gets bored out of her mind.

We will have a blast even if no one sees each other during the trip.

—Angelica Nevarez, Bing Long, Minoru Omura,
Emi Kimura, Noemi Delgado, Ana Osytek (adults)

4 Adverb poem

Teaching points: Adverbs
                      Dictionary skills
                      Thesaurus usage

The adverb poem is similar to the adjective poem in form in that it consists of six lines developing a series of adverbs to describe a single action.

Radio
Radio plays loudly
Radio plays loudly, brightly
Plays loudly, brightly, wildly
Loudly, brightly, wildly, energetically
When the music rocks.

Moon
Moon glows softly
Moon glows softly, silvery
Glows softly, silvery, soothingly
Softly, silvery, soothingly, sleepily
At night.

Detective Brown
Detective Brown solves mysteries easily
Detective Brown solves mysteries easily, quickly
Solves mysteries easily, quickly, secretly
Easily, quickly, secretly, truthfully
As part of his job.

Pattern

> Line 1: Noun
> Line 2: Same noun + verb + adverb 1
> Line 3: Same noun + verb + adverb 1, adverb 2
> Line 4: Verb + adverb 1, adverb 2, adverb 3
> Line 5: Adverb 1, adverb 2, adverb 3, adverb 4
> Line 6: Phrase or clause showing condition, time, or place

What to do

1. Ask students what adverbs do (describe an action verb or an adjective or another adverb). If students are hesitant, ask them to give some verbs that tell what they are going to do this weekend. One class suggested:

> eat
> play
> sleep
> watch TV
> shop

Then ask them how they are going to do those things, leading them to adverbs. For instance, with help from the teacher, the class suggested:

> eat often
> play with a lot of energy
> sleep soundly
> watch TV in comfort
> shop with enthusiasm

Using the student-suggested words, show the students how to create adverbs with *-ly* at the end of an adjective or by changing a noun into an adjective and then adding the -y ending (e.g., *energy* becomes *energetic* becomes *energetically*). Include additional words that show how y changes to i (*pretty* becomes *prettily*). Also point out adverbs that do not use *-ly* (e.g., *often, fast, very,* and *high.*) The list would then end up like this:

> eat often
> play energetically
> sleep soundly
> watch TV comfortably
> shop enthusiastically

This is a good opportunity to introduce dictionary skills because the adverbial form of a word is usually located after the adjective entry or as part of it, or it is in close proximity to the stem (root word).

2. Explain that students will be writing a poem that needs four adverbs for the same subject-verb stem. Show examples and, using one of the examples, have students identify the pattern, labeling the parts of speech and numbering the adverbs from 1 to 4:

Subject
Moon
Subject   verb   adverb 1
Moon glows softly
Subject   verb   adverb 1   adverb 2
Moon glows softly, silvery
Verb   adverb 1   adverb 2   adverb 3
Glows softly, silvery, soothingly
Adverb 1   adverb 2   adverb 3   adverb 4
Softly, silvery, soothingly, sleepily
Phrase showing when, where, why, or under what conditions
At night.

3. Select a subject-verb stem and ask students to help you think of other adverbs for your poem. For instance, using *a turtle crawls,* students may suggest *slowly, patiently, carefully,* or *cautiously.* Students may offer adjectives or phrases that you need to help revise into adverbs. For instance, if a student says that a turtle doesn't get tired, you would need to revise the phrase into the adverb *tirelessly.* Similarly, a suggestion that the turtle isn't in a hurry needs revising into the adverb *unhurriedly.*

4. Ask the students to select which four adverbs to use in the poem and number them 1, 2, 3, and 4.

5. Ask the students to help you place the words on the same lines as the sample and write out the first five lines of the poem:

Turtle
Turtle crawls slowly
Turtle crawls slowly, patiently
Crawls slowly, patiently, carefully
Slowly, patiently, carefully, unhurriedly

6. Ask the students for suggestions to create the last line of the poem, telling where, when, why, or under what conditions the turtle crawls this way. They might suggest:

All the time
Even when he's running
To his home
Under his shell

7. Select one of the suggestions and add it to the poem:

Turtle
Turtle crawls slowly
Turtle crawls slowly, patiently
Crawls slowly, patiently, carefully
Slowly, patiently, carefully, unhurriedly
Even when he's running.

8. Using either the student suggestions or prepared cards with subject-verb stems written on them, divide the students into small groups to write a poem together. Some topics we have used include:

Sun shines	Wolves howl	Babies cry
Cats creep	Winds blow	Birds fly
Santa Claus laughs	Water flows	Stomachs growl
Clouds hang	Ballerina dances	Clock hands move
Snow falls	Cars honk	Movie plots unwind

Note: If you object to the use of a singular noun without a determiner (e.g., *turtle* instead of *the turtle*), you might suggest that students either add the determiner or make the noun plural, if that is appropriate, as it is with *turtle* but not with *moon*.

9. Remind the students to brainstorm a list of adverbs to choose from before writing their poems. If students have difficulty thinking of more than one or two adverbs, they may want to use a thesaurus to look up one of their adverbs to get suggestions for similar words.
10. When the poems are completed, have students read them aloud to their classmates.
11. Students should now be ready to write their own individual adverb poems.

Uses

- to describe a topic within a subject area (weather phenomena, animals, mathematical concepts)
- to describe a person or character

Lesson 4

Student-written examples

Snow
Snow falls slowly
Snow falls slowly, quietly
Falls slowly, quietly, gently
Slowly, quietly, gently, beautifully
In winter.
—Nikita Rose Uy (age 7)

Bears
Bears attack ferociously
Bears attack ferociously, slowly
Attack ferociously, slowly, wildly
Ferociously, slowly, wildly, fiercely
When they're hungry.
—Antonio Arias (age 8),
Anthony Gonzales (age 8),
Davis Martinez (age 8)

Volcanoes
Volcanoes explode quickly
Volcanoes explode quickly, smokily
Explode quickly, smokily, loudly
Quickly, smokily, loudly, intensely
When they erupt.
—Noemi Torres (age 8),
Leslie Ramirez (age 8)

Motorcycles
Motorcycles race fast
Motorcycles race fast, speedily
Race fast, speedily, dangerously
Fast, speedily dangerously, gracefully
In the street.
—Benyam Hailemariam (age 13),
Debbie Ruiz (age 12)

Telephone
Telephone rings loudly
Telephone rings loudly, often
Rings loudly, often, clearly
Loudly, often, clearly, emphatically
When my boyfriend calls.
—Monica Alvarez (age 12),
Karen Montiel (age 13),
Erika Merlos (age 13)

Sun
Sun shines energetically
Sun shines energetically, softly
Shines energetically, softly, warmly
Energetically, softly, warmly, brightly
In the morning.
—Oscar Morales (age 17),
Oscar Miranda (age 16),
Mariano Alba (age 15)

Cats
Cats creep slowly
Cats creep slowly, quietly
Creep slowly, quietly, sneakily
Slowly, quietly, sneakily, nimbly
To catch the mice.
—Pragnesh Patel (age 16),
Joseph Pak (age 16),
Alejandro Castillo (age 16)

Cars
Cars honk rapidly
Cars honk rapidly, loudly
Rapidly, loudly, annoyingly
Rapidly, loudly, annoyingly, disturbingly
In the street.
—Mario Vasquez (age 14),
Jose Gomez (age 15),
Juan Jurado (age 16)

Nasty wigs
Nasty wigs stick to bald heads tenaciously
Nasty wigs stick to bald heads tenaciously, desperately
Stick to bald heads tenaciously, desperately, pretentiously
Tenaciously, desperately, pretentiously, furiously
When caught by the wind.
—Marta Oliveira, George Bassitt Jr. (adults)

Politicians
Politicians speak powerfully
Politicians speak powerfully, loudly
Speak powerfully, loudly, insistently
Powerfully, loudly, insistently, falsely
In Congress.
—Kyung-Joon Kim (adult)

Clock hands
Clock hands move alone
Clock hands move alone, quickly
Move alone, quickly, softly
Alone, quickly, softly, intricately
Every second forever
—Jessica Munguia, Emi Sugiyama (adults)

5 Alphabet poem

Teaching points: Order of letters in the alphabet
Parts of speech, phrases, or sentence structure
Dictionary usage

The simplest of all poetic forms, the alphabet poem can be made as sophisticated as needed to match the linguistic competence of your students. Letter order is the foundation for work in vocabulary, phrasing, and sentence structure. Writing alphabet poems presents a good opportunity for focused use of the dictionary and the thesaurus.

Things in my toy box
Angels
Balls
Comic books
Dragons
Electric train
Football
Godzilla tape
Helmet
Ice skates
Jump rope
Kite
Lifesaver candies
Monopoly game
Nickel collection
Ouija board
Pokemon figures
Quartz stone
Railroad tracks
Snakes made of rubber
Tablet
Unicorn
Valentines
Wickets
Xylophone
Yoyo
Zoo animals

What I did last summer
Argued about my short haircut
Baked cookies with Mom
Called my friends twice a day
Daydreamed a lot
E-mailed my friends
Floated on my air mattress in the pool
Gave all my old clothes away
Hiked to the top of Mount Rainier
Insisted on having my way
Judged my dad when I had no right
Knew I was wrong
Licked ice-cream cones daily
Made tons of new friends at the lake
Navigated the Internet
Ordered pizza for the girl I baby-sat
Pasted pictures in my scrapbook
Questioned my parents' rules
Rested, rested, and rested
Scratched my mosquito bites
Told Paul I loved him
Urged my dad to give Paul a chance
Vowed to be true forever
Wondered why I was missing school
X'd boxes on college applications
Yearned for something to do
Zigzagged around the yard

Pattern

> Select a theme and write it as the title at the top center of the paper (as has been done below). Beginning with "A," write the letters of the alphabet (one per line) down the left margin of the paper.
>
> ### "What I did on my summer vacation"
>
> **A** (select a word, phrase, or sentence beginning with the letter and corresponding to the theme)
>
> **B** (select a word, phrase, or sentence beginning with the second letter and corresponding to the theme)
>
> **C** (select a word, phrase, or sentence beginning with the third letter . . .)
>
> **D** (select a word, phrase, or sentence beginning with the fourth letter . . .)
>
> Continue the pattern for each letter of the alphabet.
>
> *Note:* It is not absolutely necessary to complete the entire alphabet.

What to do

1. Ask students whether they know the English alphabet. When they say they do, tell them that they are going to write a poem based on the alphabet, but all the lines will be based on a single theme or idea.
2. Show students sample poems with the type of lines you will use (nouns, phrases, or sentences) and have them identify the grammar of each line (nouns, phrases, or sentences).
3. Ask students to help you select a concept or theme that is relevant to something they have been studying as a class, that is part of their life experience, or just something that interests them. For students at a lower level of proficiency, you might want to guide them in selecting a topic that can be described by nouns as this kind of alphabet poem makes it easy to generate vocabulary.
4. For whatever part of speech, type of phrase, or other syntax you will use, ask students to generate some examples to make sure they understand both the grammar and the theme or topic selected. One class decided to write about the school and generated words such as:

Teachers
Students
Desks

Tell the students that those words are good examples of items for the lines that begin with the letters *t*, *s*, and *d*, but with some adjectives to make them noun phrases they can also be used for the letters *g*, *f*, and *b*:

> Good teachers
> Friendly students
> Brown desks

5. Divide the class into groups of three or four students each. Make sure that each group has a dictionary to use so that the groups can browse through it to look for words starting with the letter(s) they will be assigned. Give each group a felt pen and several strips of paper or cardboard (about 20 inches by 4 inches). Each strip will have a letter of the alphabet on the left side of it. Pass out the strips randomly until all twenty-six strips have been distributed to the groups.

6. Remind the students that they are creating a poem made up of words (or phrases or sentences, depending on the level of the students) that begin with each letter of the alphabet and that will be about the topic they have selected. If you have determined a particular grammar structure they should use, remind them to be grammatically consistent. For example, if the poem is going to be a series of nouns or noun phrases describing the concept, then each line should follow suit. If, on the other hand, each line is a verb phrase describing the concept, then each line should be a verb phrase.

7. Ask students to visualize the concept in their minds and to select appropriate descriptive words, phrases, or sentences beginning with the letters they have been assigned. This is a good opportunity to reinforce dictionary skills. In fact, you may want to select a letter and model the process of scanning the dictionary for specific words.

8. Instruct students that as they come up with the lines of the poem, they should write them on the strips you have given them so that the complete poem can be assembled with the whole group.

9. Assemble the poem by having the students post the strips in the proper alphabetic sequence. If you have written the alphabet on the board in columns while the students were writing, groups will be able to post their own lines quickly as they finish them.

10. Because the groups do not know what other groups have written until the entire poem is assembled, there may be duplicate ideas. This provides a good opportunity to show students how and why to revise first drafts.

11. With the group poem on display, take the opportunity to have students do a choral reading of the poem.

12. Students are now ready to write other alphabet poems on different topics. Because this poem is so long and requires varied vocabulary about a single topic, it is best done in small groups rather than individually.

Uses

- to practice the order of letters in the alphabet
- to review vocabulary in content-related areas: animals, seasons, events, history, locations, mathematics, and so on
- to summarize the plot or describe a character in a book the student has read

Student-written examples

Things in the rain forest
Anteater
Birds
Crocodile
Drops
Eagle
Flowers
Green
Harpy eagle
Iguana
Jaguar
Kapok tree
Leopard
Monkey
Noise
Okapi
Panther
Quetzal
Rabbit
Snake
Tiger
Understory
Vine
Water
X-ray fish
Yapok
Zebra
—Elizabeth Gordon Taylor's class (ages 6 and 7)

Christmastime

A is for all the fun we had on Christmas Day opening the presents.
B is for the birthday of my aunt Michelle on December 9.
C is for Christmas games, spirit, and joy.
D is for the delightful happiness on Christmas Day.
E is for the excitement of this time of year.
F is for my favorite uncles and aunts who came to visit.
G is for the gifts that I got for being so good.
H is for the happy holiday over track break.
I is for the ice-cream maker I received.
J is for the joyful holiday that passed by quickly.
K is for the karaoke I did: Britney Spears' "Hit Me Baby."
L is for Luxor where I went to see *Fantasia 2000*.
M is for movies I saw over Christmas break.
N is for the *Nutcracker* I saw with beautiful ballerinas.
O is for the outfits I got for Christmas.
P is for the presents I opened on Christmas Day.
Q is for the Queen Makela with her wand.
R is for the restaurant I went to at the Mandalay Bay.
S is for *Stuart Little,* who I saw at the movies.
T is for the turkey I ate for Christmas dinner.
U is for under the tree where all the presents were stacked.
V is for the visitors who came for Christmas from New England.
W is for winter fun that lasted all through Christmas break.
X is for the xylophone that baby Emily played with.
Y is for the yellow snow cone I made with my snow cone maker.
Z is for zoom, how the time passed by so quickly.
—Abella Rutahindurwa (age 9)

Math is . . .
Angry addition that increases
Basic brackets that hold numbers
Competitive conversions that are complicated
Dirty decimals that split whole numbers
Even numbers that can be divided by two
Filthy fractions that are sometimes confusing
Great geometry that is based on points, planes, and lines
Happy hypothesis that makes for logical conclusions
Improbable inverses that are usually false
Jammed junctions that are muddling and befuddling
Kind kilowatts that keep the TVs running
Long lines that go on forever
Merciful metric system that makes measurement easy
Negative numbers that are sometimes degrading
Outstanding octagons that have eight sides
Powerful primes that other numbers can't touch
Quirky quadrilaterals that are four-sided polygons
Rotary reciprocals that are opposites of other numbers
Scary subtraction that decreases in size
Tricky trigonometry that is made of triangles
Universal units that could be any number
Vertical line that intersects horizontals
Wonderful word problems that either decrease or increase
X-citing x-axis that coordinates points
Yellow yardsticks that measure distance
Zany zeroes that are really nothing
—Traci Begay (age 12)

Things at the park
Ants that crawl on my picnic blanket
Birds that sing and fly
Cars that wait in the parking lot
Dogs chasing after balls
Everyone happy and having fun
Flowers that smell so sweet
Grass that tickles your feet
Hills for riding our bikes up and down
Ice-cream cones from the Tastee Freeze truck
Jump ropes crossing and moving in a circle
Kids playing soccer
Lakes where fish and ducks go swimming
Musicians that play for dancing
Nests holding baby birds
Old people sleeping in the park
Playgrounds for little kids
Queen bees that bite and sting
Rabbits with their babies
Swimming pools for children only
Trees standing tall in the wind
Umbrellas that cover our heads
Visitors talking together
Water splashing in the fountains
X-treme frisbee being played with dogs and friends
Yo-yos that go up and down on a string
Zones for playing volleyball
—Pat Arroyo's class (ages 11 to 13)

Our school
Auditorium
Big basketball players
Cold hallways
Daily work
Exercise center
French fries at lunch
Good grades
Happy students
I love LVHS stickers
Jackets with letters
Keys to the school
Language class
My favorite friends
Nice teachers
Open doors
Principal's office
Quick learners
Room 828
Soccer balls
Tough security guards
Unusual hair colors
Volleyball nets
Wildcat people
"**X**" on my test
Yellow school bus
Zero errors
– Claudette Willems's class (ages 14 to 17)

Reasons we like and need to learn English
Always able to understand Bruce Springsteen songs
Books are easier to read
Canadians can understand me
Days are shorter when we learn
English is a common language
Finding friends is easier
Grammar is a long topic to learn
Help me! I must learn English!
I love English Language Center
Jobs are easier to find when you know it
Kids can talk it, so why can't I?
Library has lots of books in English
Money comes from learning the language
Never is too late to learn
Oh, how nice is our teacher!
Portuguese, Japanese, French, and Spanish languages are cute, but we
    enjoy English!
Question the essence of life
Red, purple, yellow, green – all these colors will take you to the
    English rainbow
Silver dreams of new opportunities
To meet a challenge
Unique feelings of making yourself understood
Visualize yourself interacting as a regular person
We are making new friends
"X"cellent job opportunities
Yes! We really can speak English
Zealous love of language
—Marta Oliveira, George Bassitt Jr., Kyung-Joon Kim,
   Susana Gonzalez, Kat Zdeb Toczynska, Mosammat Khanom,
   Jessica Munguia, Emi Sugiyama (adults)

6 Beginnings and endings poem

Teaching points: Exclamatory statement
Opposites
Contrast

The beginnings and endings poem is generally five lines long and made up of four exclamatory statements and a brief summary. Lines 1 and 3 are thematically related. Lines 2 and 4 are also thematically related but provide a mirror image of lines 1 and 3. The poem is useful for thinking about and describing contrasts or change. The last line ties the poem together by repeating one word three times, a word that describes the dominant concept of the poem.

Farewell to overcoats.
Hello to tennis lessons.
Farewell to rainy days.
Hello to sunshine.
It's spring, spring, spring.

Yes to good marks on my homework.
No to getting in trouble.
Yes to being on time to class.
No to making excuses.
It's success, success, success!

Good-bye to rags of clothing.
Hello to gowns and jewels.
Good-bye to ugly stepsisters.
Hello to a handsome prince.
Cinderella has met her love, love, love.

Patterns

Farewell to _____ . Hello to _____ . Farewell to _____ . Hello to _____ . It's _____, _____, _____ .	Yes to _____ . No to _____ . Yes to _____ . No to _____ . It's _____, _____, _____ .

What to do

1. Divide the students into two groups. Tell them that each group will be brainstorming ideas for a single poem by the whole class. Give each group a piece of paper or note card that has one word written on it. The two words should be contrasting concepts or the beginning and ending of a cycle. For instance, one group might have the word *school* while the other group has the word *vacation*. Give the students about 5 minutes to write down things associated with their group's word. The "school" group might think of such words as *books, teachers, tests, studying,* while the "vacation" group might have such words as *swimming, summer camp, baseball, picnics.*

2. Show samples of the poem to the students and ask them to identify the pattern, noting the contrasting lines, the repetition of the first word in alternate lines, the repetition in the final line, and the punctuation.

3. Ask the students for some of the ideas they wrote down to begin writing the poem as a whole class. Remind them that since they did not know what the pattern was before they wrote down their ideas, they may want to revise the wording to make it fit the poem better. Write the poem on the board or on an overhead projector.

4. To emphasize the contrast, use choral response to read it aloud. Dividing the entire group into two again, have one group read aloud one set of lines (*Farewell* or *Yes* lines) while the other group responds aloud with the intervening set of lines (*Hello* or *No* lines). Both groups then read aloud the final line together.

5. Ask students to think of other topics that contrast, occur in cycles, or go through a metamorphosis. Write their suggestions on the board. Some topics might include day/night, summer/fall (or any other seasonal change), war/peace, laughing/crying, happiness/sadness, healthy food/junk food. Students can use these topics or think of others to write their own beginnings and endings poem in small groups.

6. Have the students share their poems by reading them aloud in the same choral response mode used with the class poem.

7. They should now be ready to write their own beginnings and endings poems.

Uses

- to chronicle the beginning and ending of a given cycle (such as seasons or divisions of a day)
- to contrast opposing concepts (such as war/peace or day/night)

- to describe changes that occur in nature, people, or development of inanimate objects or more abstract concepts (such as a seed becoming a flower, a character changing his or her life, or an uninhabited area becoming a city)

Variations

1. The beginnings and endings poem, although very useful for identifying the contrast in seasons or other natural events, can also signify the start and stop or the contrast of more personal experiences. The beginning of each stem can be altered to express the writer's experience.

Begin eating low-fat dinners.
Stop smoking two packs a day.
Begin hitting the gym after work.
Stop snacking on salt-filled treats.
It's skinny, skinny, skinny!

Cry when my big sister hits me.
Smile when my daddy comes
    home.
Cry when mommy sends me to
    bed so early.
Smile when my puppy licks my
    nose.
It's family, family, family!

2. The last line of the poem may also be altered:

Good-bye to textbooks.
Hello to lazy days.
Good-bye to teachers' rules.
Hello to friends and games.
School is out, out, out!

Student-written examples

The butterfly
Good-bye to furry, fat, green bodies.
Hello to thin, powdery, colorful
    wings.
Good-bye to slowly crawling.
Hello to graceful flight.
The butterfly has come out, out,
    out of its cocoon!
—Karen Callahan's class
    (ages 9 and 10)

School
Farewell to sleeping late.
Hello to school.
Farewell to my friends.
Hello to my teachers.
School has started, started, started!
—Aileen Ruiz (age 13)

Vacation
Yes to the last day of school.
No to homework and teachers.
Yes to playing in the amusement arcade.
No to sitting still in class all day.
It's Friday, Friday, Friday!
—Claudette Willems's class
    (ages 14 to 17)

Diet results
Farewell to being fat.
Hello to being thin.
Farewell to walking light.
Hello to beautiful clothes.
It's success, success, success!
—Rosa Pacheco (adult)

Crime
Farewell to gangs and violence.
Hello to parents and teachers with their words of advice.
Farewell to drugs and addiction.
Hello to friends and family.
It's no more robbery, death, accidents!
—Aurora Rolon (adult)

Debt-free
Farewell to bills and debts.
Hello to days without pressure or obligations.
Farewell to the bill collectors that follow me.
Hello to happy days with my family.
The debts are paid, paid, paid!
—Juan Lopez (adult)

Peace
Farewell to nuclear armies of the world.
Hello to dialogue and understanding.
Farewell to war and death.
Hello to enjoying the days of the spiritual light.
It's peace, peace, peace!
–Cesar Garcia (adult)

7 Biopoem

Teaching points: Adjectives
Relative clauses
Items in a series

Using a series of adjectives, relative clauses, and items in series, the biopoem briefly summarizes the life of anyone or anything. It can be based on personal knowledge, but it can also be a creative showcase for research on people, plants, or animals.

Natasha
Carefree, happy, crazy, lazy
Sister of no one
Lover of guys, dancing, summertime, and swimsuits
Who feels happy when school is over, sad when she can't go to movies,
    and strange when she's being serious
Who needs clothes from The Gap, attention, and good grades
Who fears failing English, being lonely, and giving a report in front of
    the whole class
Who gives phone calls, notes, and presents to friends
Who would like to see herself become rich, famous, and successful
Resident of Nevada
Bailia

Abraham
Honest, able, intelligent, humble
Husband of Mary Todd
Lover of freedom, justice, and peace
Who felt destined to make history, determined to free the slaves,
    dedicated to make men equal
Who needed to make people listen, win the war, reunite the country
Who feared the hatred in men's eyes, ignorance bred by prejudice,
    social injustice
Who gave his dreams, his hope, and his life
Who would have liked to have had more days
Resident of the White House
Lincoln

Pattern

Line 1:	First name
Line 2:	Four traits that describe the character
Line 3:	Relative of _____ (brother, sister, daughter, etc.)
Line 4:	Lover of _____ (list three people, things, or ideas)
Line 5:	Who feels _____ (three emotions)
Line 6:	Who needs _____ (three items)
Line 7:	Who fears _____ (three items)
Line 8:	Who gives _____ (three items)
Line 9:	Who would like to see _____ (three items)
Line 10:	Resident of _____
Line 11:	Last name

What to do

1. Show students some sample poems and then show them the pattern, leaving it on the board for the rest of the activity. Tell them that you are going to create one together and ask for suggestions of someone or something they all know about. Select one of the topics.
2. Have prepared strips of paper or cardboard (about 20 inches by 4 inches) numbered 1 through 11 (one for each line of the poem). Write the subject's first name on strip 1 and tape it to the wall. Write the last name on strip 11.
3. Divide the class into small groups, giving each one a numbered strip. Each group will write the line that corresponds to the number of the strip. When the groups finish the poem, assemble it on the wall underneath the first line. Add the last line (strip 11).
4. Read the poem aloud and ask students whether there are any parts that should be revised or edited; enter revisions on the posted strips.
5. Students are now ready to write their own poems, either individually for personal poems, or in pairs or small groups for poems about someone or something else.

Note: For a personal biopoem, we have found that using a web (like the one below) to brainstorm before writing allows students to see themes that help create a more unified poem. The web can be adapted for historical or famous figures or fictional characters as well as for plants, animals, or abstract concepts. In all cases, the pattern should remain visible for the students to consult as they transform their ideas into the lines of the poem.

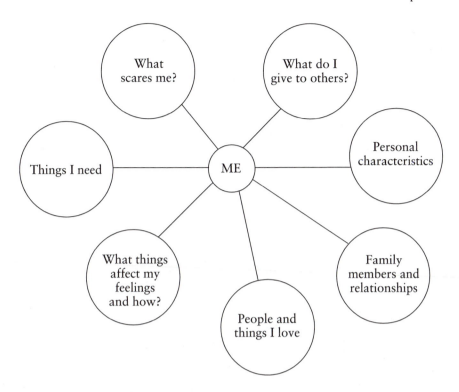

Uses

- to conceptualize a historical figure
- to explore or personify an inanimate object
- to imagine the life of an animal or a plant
- to personalize a character in a book
- to give life to an abstract concept
- to reflect on one's self (could be used as an icebreaker in the first days of class)

Lesson 7

Student-written examples

Windy
Loving, inquisitive, kind, funny
Daughter to Lai Yin, Yum Shing Wong, sister to Simon
Lover of my family, vegetables, homework
Who feels air, grateful, and happy
Who fears T. rex, ghosts, and Frankenstein
Who gives my heart, my help, and my time
Who would like to see the inside of my body, the moon up close, and
    the inside of a spaceship
Resident of Las Vegas
Wong
—Windy Wong (age 7)

Carlos
Nice, kind, friendly, and intelligent
Brother of sister Ana
Lover of family, uncles, and aunts
Who feels happy to have friends, a dog, and food
Who needs school, water, and clothes
Who fears getting F's, trouble, and death
Who gives letters, money, and a helping hand
Who would like to see his parents, cousins, and his dog
Piza
—Luis Valdovinos (age 9)

Algebraic
Algebraic equations, desired answers, several keys
Sibling to no one
Lover of numbers, symbols, and words
Who feels happy when work is done, upset when grades are bad,
    and mad when problems are hard
Who needs problems, answers, and phrases
Who fears failing math, having wrong answers, and running out of
    paper plus problems to work on
Who gives knowledge, numbers, and problems
Who would like to see people learning, working, and
    understanding math
Resident of algebraic sentences
Phrases
—Sheadeen Nez (age 13)

Rose
Colorful, aromatic, pretty
Sister to gardenias, sunflowers, and daisies
Lover of parties, weddings, and dates
Who feels warm in the sun, hurt when cut, and satisfied when it rains
Who needs water, sun, and dirt
Who fears drought, chemicals, and scissors
Who gives love, happiness, and peace
Who would like to see all people happy
Resident of beautiful gardens
Linda
—Karla Chacon (age 15), Moses Araujo (age 16),
    Joel Bejarano (age 16)

Pancho
Strong, warrior, brave, and smart
Son of a farmer
Lover of justice, freedom, and respect
Who felt angry to see his precious people as slaves, abused,
    disrespected, and killed
Who needed money, followers, and the support of the people to fight
    for liberty
Who feared to lose his people, their rights, and the war against
    rich people
Who gave his life and dedication
Who would liked to have seen his nation free, independent, and
    respected
Resident of Durango, Mexico
Villa
—Francisco Tlatelpa (age 14), Rafael Pena (age 16),
    Cesar Gonzalez (age 16)

Pacific
Clean, huge, blue
Grandfather of Asia, South America, and North America
Who feels wanted by all
Who needs to be clean
Who fears pollution
Who gives a lot of fun, food, and sport
Who would like to see less dumping of trash and chemicals
Resident of half of the world
Ocean
—Maribel Esqueda (age 14), PeeJay Tagudin (age 16),
    Ivis Cruz-Antunez (age 15), Melisa Cejas (age 14)

Cappuccino
Sweet, relaxing, warm, bright
Relative of caffe latte, mocha, American coffee
Lover of adult people
Who feels a clean heart, bright eyes, smiling face
Who needs students, businesspeople, everybody
Who fears tea, milk, juice
Who gives mothers, fathers, and coffee makers joy, energy,
    and a wonderful time
Who would like to see all the world's people drinking
Resident of my table
Liquid love
—Unyoung Son (adult)

Toby
Tiny, playful, lovely, energetic
Brother of Pomeranians and Bichon-frise
Lover of toys, kisses, tricks
Who feels sad when he is alone, excited when someone comes home,
    furious when a stranger is close
Who needs to be spoiled, groomed, fed
Who fears German Shepherds, Dobermans, Rottweilers
Who gives company, loud barks, lots of hair
Who would like to see cheese in his food, shoes all over the floor,
    no veterinarian near him
Resident of the world
De la Bamba
—Susana Gonzalez (adult)

Peter
Lovely, playful, heavy eater
Lover of my family
Who feels lonely when no one is at home
Who needs Mew Chops and bill-cutter
Who likes sunshine, water balloons, flying bees
Who fears the trash car, little boys, thunder
Who would like to step on the window sill
Resident of a green house
Sweet little cat
Moon
—Hyesook Moon (adult)

8　Blotz poem

Teaching points:　Vocabulary
Dictionary skills
Alliteration

The blotz poem encourages students to use imagination in order to make up a creature that does strange, nonsensical things. It also helps students practice using the dictionary in order to produce the alliteration the poem calls for.

This is a teacherian.
Teacherians live in Turkish towers on top of telegraph transmitters in Tibet.
Teacherians eat tortoise toes, tangy tarts, tender toast, and tuna.
Teacherians throw temper tantrums, torment students, try on toupees, and twiddle their thumbs.
Teacherians teach trigonometry, enjoy tapestry, and like tanning their temples.
This teacherian told me to tape up my mouth. It tortured me and tore out my teeth.

Pattern

> Line 1: Name your creature (This is a . . .).
> Line 2: Tell where your creature lives (using four or more words that begin with the same beginning sound of the creature's name).
> Line 3: Tell what your creature eats (using four or more words that begin with the same beginning sound of the creature's name).
> Line 4: Tell what your creature likes (using four or more words that begin with the same beginning sound of the creature's name).
> Line 5: Tell something about your creature (using three or more words that begin with the same beginning sound of the creature's name).
> Line 6: Tell something about what your creature did to you (using three or more words that begin with the same beginning sound of the creature's name).

What to do

1. To introduce the concept of alliteration, make a game board grid that has topics (such as foods, colors, places) down the left side and letters of the alphabet across the top:

	p	b	g	h	w
food					
colors					
places					
cars					
sports					

2. Give students 4 to 5 minutes to try to fill in the grid with items that fit the topic and begin with the letters selected. For instance, the row of food might include *pickle, banana, grape, ham,* and *watermelon.* Because of the pressure of time, students will probably not be able to fill in all the boxes individually, but as a class they will probably be able to fill in all the boxes for the next step.

3. Using the students' information, fill in the grid on the board, going across the rows:

	p	b	g	h	w
food	pickle pasta	banana beef	grapes gum	ham honey	watermelon
colors	pink purple	brown beige	green gold	harvest gold	white
places	Paris Phoenix	Beirut Boston	Grand Canyon	Harlem Hawaii	Wichita Wales
cars	Porsche Peugeot	buggy	Grand Am	Honda	wagon
sports	Ping-Pong polo	baseball bowling	golf	hockey	water polo

4. Have students help make up a nonsense sentence using a word from each topic in a single column: "Paul likes to eat purple pasta in his Porsche on his way to a Ping-Pong game in Paris." Explain that the sentence they have just created using words that start with the same sound is an example of alliteration. Also explain that the game required them to use the same letter for starting each word but that alliteration is based on sound, not letters. Therefore, phrases such as "foreign phone" or "king of chemistry" are also alliterative.
5. Introduce the blotz poem by explaining that it is a nonsense poem based on alliteration about an imaginary creature. Show the students some samples and then the pattern.
6. Make up the name of a creature and create the first line as an example. Then have students help you think of words for the next line. Suppose this is your creature and first line:

This is a fraggleface.
Fragglefaces live in Philadelphia, far away from fluffy foxes.

Point out that the alliterative words are not just in the names of the item (the place-name in this example) but also in phrases describing it. For the next line (what the creature eats), the students might come up with words and phrases such as:

farm fresh eggs
french fries
foreign foods
frozen fingers

From their suggestions, create that line of the poem:

Fragglefaces get full by eating fattening foods like french fries
   and frozen fudge.

7. To make sure that students understand the idea, continue as a large
   group to brainstorm ideas for each line, selecting their favorites and
   combining them into the pattern for that line. The "fraggleface"
   poem could end up something like this:

This is a fraggleface.
Fragglefaces live in Philadelphia, far away from fluffy foxes.
Fragglefaces get full by eating fattening foods like french fries
   and frozen fudge.
Fragglefaces like to fandango furiously while flattening fences
   on football fields.
This fraggleface has fuzzy fake fur on his face
And forced me to fill my flask with a frothy, fruit-flavored
   milkshake.

8. Divide students into pairs or small groups to work on their own
   poems. You may want to suggest some possible names for creatures.
   We have used such made-up words as:

Dragonardo	Stiggybot
Hugabug	Bumbledytop
Terriformous	Galumphorus
Denderanium	Rackosaurus

Note: Younger students seem to have more difficulty with made-up
creatures. Instead, you might suggest that they create an alliterative
name to go with a real animal (e.g., Sammy Seal, Pedro Poodle).

9. Encourage students to use a dictionary to find words that start with
   the sounds they need for their poems.
10. Have students share their poems by reading them aloud.

Uses

- to culminate a dictionary and/or thesaurus unit with a fun "test"
- to accompany drawings of imaginary and mythical creatures
- to practice pronunciation of difficult sounds

Student-written examples

This is Kathy Cat.
Kathy Cat lives in a candy castle with her crocodiles in California.
Kathy Cat eats corn nuts, cabbage, and cotton candy.
Kathy Cat can do cartwheels while crunching colorful carrots.
Kathy Cat carries her cars to Kansas and Colorado.
Kathy Cat can be cool with crowds at carnivals.
Kathy Cat has a colorful cape that can make her cozy in candy land.
Kathy Cat crashed her coral car into me and caused a huge
    catastrophe.
—Xochitl Nava (age 9)

This is a Bugaboo.
Bugaboos live on baking beaches off the Bay of Bengal.
Bugaboos eat bacon, beef, bologna, burgers, bread, and especially bugs.
Bugaboos like to bake gingerbread, play basketball and baseball,
    and squish bombing bugs.
Bugaboos teach biology, ride bicycles, play with butter, and draw
    blonde babes.
This Bugaboo bleached our beautiful bodacious hair and baked us
    burgers with bacon.
—Miriam Rodriguez (age 13), Azalia Rivera (age 13)

This is a Nanoid.
Nanoids live in narrow, noisy neighborhoods in Nevada.
Nanoids eat natural, native nectarines from Nebraska, neon newts,
    and a nut full of nightingales.
Nanoids like to be near nonrenewable, neat nests and wear navy
    nightgowns.
Nanoids are noisy, nagging, nervous, and narcotic.
This Nanoid neglected Nga's need to be noticed in a nice, noisy nation.
—Christy Luanglath (age 13), Nga Ngo (age 13)

This is a stiggybot.
Stiggybots live in small stinky sandcastles south of San Francisco.
Stiggybots savor salty salmon sandwiches with strawberry soup
    and shrimp salad.
Stiggybots like to swim in the sea in summer and ski on shiny snowy
    slopes in winter.
Stiggybots are extremely stupid, silly, sinful, scornful strangers.
This stiggybot scared us when she screamed while slinging slimy
    spaghetti on our shoes.
—Joannie Monroy's class (ages 14 to 17)

This is a Trollusk.
Trollusks live in Torreon but are often transported to Texas, Toronto, and Tennessee.
Trollusks eat turkey, tomatoes, tortas, tacos, tostados, and toasted Twinkies.
Trollusks like toys, tigers, trucks, telephones, and taxis.
Trollusks talk a lot.
Trollusks do traditional things like tournaments and tracing to have fun.
This Trollusk told my parents that I told him that I told my true friend that I like Trollusks.
—Bertha Hernandez (age 15), Denise Hernandez (age 15),
   Leonardo Cejas (age 14), Elizabeth Caro (age 15)

This is a Rektilogo.
Rektilogos live in rumbling rocks around rivers.
Rektilogos eat raw rabbits, rice, rats, and ragged rags.
Rektilogos like railways, rainstorms, and refreshments but refuse rules.
Rektilogos raid with razzmatazz reggae and recriminating redemption.
This Rektilogo redeveloped my roots, reduced my refectory, ran over me, and ripped my wrists.
—Francisco Tlatlpa (age 14), Rafael Pena (age 16),
   Cesar Gonzalez (age 16)

This is a Cancong.
Cancongs live in old castles with cockroaches and scary cats.
Cancongs eat devil's cake and corncobs with cocoa.
Cancongs like to catch crazy green-eyed cats.
Cancongs are cool, creative, but careless creatures.
This Cancong makes me feel cozy and comfortable but drives me crazy sometimes.
—Cristina Paredes (age 15), Katy Martinez (age 15),
   Jose Alvarado (age 16)

This is a Dragonando.
Dragonandos live at the dead-end dwelling where the drunk driver died.
Dragonandos eat dogs and donkeys dipped in dew with a double deer for dessert.
Dragonandos like to daydream and drink daiquiris while dancing the dragarena.
Dragonandos are dirty and disgusting, yet darling and defenseless.
This Dragonando dragged me out of my dreadful dream and disappeared with the dawn.
—Galina Petrova (adult)

9 Catalog poem

Teaching points: Verbs
Nouns
Phrases
Classifying

Catalog verse focuses on listing verbs, nouns, and phrases to describe a category of items. The last line tells what the category is.

Jumping	Stores	Hands that move
Running	Houses	Numbers that count
Laughing	Apartments	Bells that ring
Crying	Offices	Chimes that clang
Skating	Sidewalks	Alarms that buzz
Rolling	Buses	These are the clocks in my
Giggling	Pedestrians	house.
Eating	Cars	
Playing	Trains	
Growing	This is my city.	
Kids, kids, kids!		

Pattern

Verb	Noun	Phrase
Verb	Noun	Phrase
Verb	Noun	Phrase
Verb	Noun	Phrase
Verb	Noun	Phrase
Verb	Noun	Phrase
Category, category, category	This is . . .	These are . . .

What to do

1. Show the students some sample poems, one at a time, but cover up the final line. Ask them whether they can guess what each poem is about.
2. Ask students to point out what parts of speech are used in the different sample poems. For the poems at the beginning of this lesson, they would identify verbs (present participles), nouns, and noun phrases.
3. Ask students to notice the different patterns of the last line in each poem, and explain that these variations can be interchangeable. Their choice of pattern depends on their own preference.
4. Have students generate a list of topics with which they are familiar. Select one.
5. Ask students to name verbs (or whatever part of speech you're working on) that describe the topic (how it moves, what it does, or what elements it includes). Write their words on the board in list form.
6. If you're working with verbs, then asking what the topic does or how it moves will probably elicit verbs in the simple present tense (run, play, walk, etc.). Either add the – *ing* ending or use this opportunity to teach the spelling changes that occur when adding -*ing*.
7. With the list in place on the board, add the final line by writing the topic three times.
8. Divide the class into small groups and have each group create its own poem. If students need help with deciding on topics, you might want to provide them with ideas by writing the last line of the poem on cards and handing them out to the groups. Some suggestions we have used include:

cars	birds	things at the beach
hair	fathers	things in our school
doctors	eyes	things in my closet
mothers	water	things at the park
spring		

9. When the students finish their poems, ask each group to read its list and let the other students guess what the final line (topic) is. If the other students cannot guess the topic, then encourage them to help the group add verbs that will describe the topic better.

Uses

- to check for understanding of a particular part of speech
- to play as a game to see which words best describe a topic
- to extend or enlarge vocabulary

Student-written examples

Barking
Growling
Playing
Running
Leaping
Chasing
Sleeping
Smelling
Scratching
Licking
Loving
Dogs, dogs, dogs!
—Mikojai Kopacz (age 5)

Wheels
Brakes
Seat
Pedals
Handlebars
Chains
Lights
Horn
Bike, bike, bike!
—Alexis Gomez (age 8)

Computer
Desks
Books
Lights
Door
Posters
Carpet
Backpacks
Board
Chairs
TV
Window
This is our classroom.
—Luis De Oleo (age 11), Marco Tamayo (age 12),
    Francisco Chirino (age 11), Natalia Oliveros (age 13),
    Yulimi Castaneda (age 12)

Mangoes
Monkeys
Snakes
Trees
Beetles
Toucans
Sloths
Butterflies
Turtles
Tigers
Jungle, jungle, jungle!
—Antonio Arias (age 8),
    Abraham Rodriguez (age 8)

Screaming
Yelling
Hitting
Scratching
Pushing
Stabbing
Kicking
Bleeding
Crying
Punching
Fight, fight, fight!
—Viridiana Trujillo (age 11)

Waving
Writing
Touching
Clapping
Brushing
Playing
Holding
Slapping
Driving
Painting
Pointing
Hands, hands, hands!
—Juan Ramirez (age 15),
    Karim Ojeda (age 14),
    Maira Flores (age 16)

People swimming
Water moving
Children playing
Beach balls bouncing
Sand blowing
Waves crashing
Bathing suits showing
Volleyball tossing
These are things at the beach.
—Jhoselyn Alfaro (age 15),
    Arturo Smith (age 15),
    Marcos Martinez (age 15)

Showers
Mud
Tears
Rivers
Ocean
Lake
Rain
Lagoon
Puddles
Water, water water!
—Gerson Huertero (age 15),
    Phoubeck Sithovong (age 16),
    Maria Arcos (age 15)

Ringing
Talking
Communicating
Dialing
Charging
Sounding
Voice mailing
Messaging
Forwarding
Blocking
This is what my cell phone does.
—Mariano Alba,
    Bonifacio Perez (adults)

Crying
Blinking
Looking
Seeing
Opening
Moving
Winking
Crossing
Flirting
Eyes, eyes, eyes!
—Luis Garcia, Lazaro
    Hernandez (adults)

Ordering
Guiding
Educating
Teaching
Instructing
Understanding
Loving
Helping
Fathers, fathers, fathers!
—Alejandro Perez, Rosa Adame
    (adults)

10 Cinquain

Teaching points: Nouns
Adjectives
Participles
Synonyms

By creating an image without complete sentences, the cinquain (French for "a group of five") allows students to focus on a few specific parts of speech, thereby reinforcing their understanding of grammar terms. The brevity also requires an economy of expression, emphasizing a need to refine vocabulary by selecting the best choice of words. The use of commas to separate items in a series can also be introduced or reinforced, as can capitalization of a proper noun.

Dogs
Furry, cuddly
Running, playing, barking
Always loyal and loving
Friends

Snow White
Beautiful, kind
Singing, dreaming, waiting
Until her love arrives
Princess

Pattern

Line 1: Noun
Line 2: Two adjectives
Line 3: Three present participles
Line 4: Four-word phrase
Line 5: Synonym for noun or closely related noun

What to do

1. Tell students that they're going to be writing a poem that creates a picture without using sentences. Instead, it uses different parts of speech and only parts of a sentence. Ask them to name the parts of speech they know, listing them on the board. You may also want to elicit the names for parts of a sentence, specifically subjects and phrases.

2. Show the students several sample poems. Ask them to identify the pattern by naming the parts of speech for the first three lines (noun, adjectives, present participles or – *ing* verbs). Ask them to identify the part of a sentence that makes the fourth line (phrase). Ask them about the last line, pointing out that the final noun is usually a synonym or closely related noun for the subject of the poem stated on the first line.

3. Ask students to suggest one-word topics with which they are familiar. Select one to use in creating a sample poem with the class.

4. Have students brainstorm a list of adjectives related to the topic. Write down the words so they can choose from all their options. Encourage them to select the two most appropriately descriptive words to place in the second line. As you write the two words into the poem, demonstrate the use of a comma to separate two adjectives.

5. Ask students to think of present participles to describe the topic, following the same brainstorming and selection procedure used with the adjectives. As you write the three words into the poem, demonstrate the use of a comma to separate the series of three present participles.

6. Ask students for phrases that describe the selected topic or how the topic affects them. Following the brainstorming and selection process, transfer the selected phrase to the poem.

7. Ask students for synonyms or words that are closely equivalent to the original topic. In our example about dogs, for instance, *friend* is not really a synonym for *dog,* but for some people it can be a close equivalent. The same is true for *music* and *piano.* Follow the same brainstorming and selection process as before, and then write the final line of the poem.

8. Read the completed poem aloud. Ask the students whether they want to make any changes to enhance meaning or rhythm. Allow students to negotiate changes. Edit the poem as they make suggestions and read it again.

9. Students should now be ready to begin writing their own poems as individuals, in pairs, or in small groups as the student samples illustrate.

Uses

- to introduce students to each other
- to clarify understanding of an animal, math concept, or other content-related term
- to describe a character from a story students have read
- to describe a friend, family member, or pet

- to describe a geographic place (e.g., city, state, country) or concept (e.g., home, freedom, school, love)
- to incorporate the student's native language with English in defining a word in either language

Student-written examples

Frogs
Slippery, long-legged
Eating, jumping, croaking
Sitting on lily pads
Amphibians
—Vivian Aquilar (age 7)

Roadrunner
Fast, brown
Running, hunting, searching
Eats rattlesnakes and lizards
Desert bird
—Elizabeth Gordon Taylor's
class (ages 6 and 7)

Dolphin
Gray, flippered
Waving, swimming, jumping
Lives in the ocean
Mammal
—Layla Medina (age 9)

Winnie the Pooh
Yellow, fat
Eating, playing, climbing
Lives in a tree
Bear
—Layla Medina (age 9)

Star
White, pointy
Shining, glowing, moving
In the night sky
Twinkler
—Xiomara Tejada (age 9)

Puppy
Cute, scared
Barking, eating, chewing
Likes to play around
Dog
—Adilene Fuentes (age 9),
Noemi Torres (age 9)

Leslie
Smart, athletic
Running, jumping, learning
Always on the playground
Fun
—Leslie Ramirez (age 9)

Cone
Sharp, triangular
Apexing, pointing, climaxing
Filled with ice cream
Peak
—Leanne Sam (age 12)

Teacher
Nice, helpful
Walking, writing, reading
Helping students to learn
Maestra
—Evelyn Jaime (age 11)

Superman
Strong, fast
Saving, flying, fighting
Famous celebrity in comics
Hero
—Eduardo Campos (age 16),
Jose Gomez (age 15),
Juan Jurado (age 16)

Cinderella
Sweet, pretty
Cleaning, crying, dreaming
Until she met her love
Princess
—Linhnaphone Bouaravong
(age 17), Vanhdala
Keomalavong (age 17),
Sandra Gonzalez (age 14),
Claudia Cardenas (age 15)

Las Vegas
Bright, colorful
Gambling, entertaining, thrilling
World-famous casino city
Nevada
—Pragnesh Patel (age 16),
Alejandro Castillo (age 16),
Luis Perez (age 15),
Joseph Pak (age 16)

Piano
Grand, elegant
Sparkling, feeling, brightening
Love of my life
Music
—Lok Ng (adult)

Jealousy
Dangerous, ferocious
Destroying, vanishing, perishing
Makes everything become hell
Envy
– Ming Wu (adult)

Jorge
Curious, intelligent
Listening, analyzing, evaluating
Learning to speak English
Lawyer
– Jorge Bastillos (adult)

11 Color metaphor poem

Teaching points: Vocabulary associated with colors
Sentences using the verb *to be*
Metaphors

Green is the grass
that tickles
my feet.

Green are the leaves
that hold
the red rose.

Green is the skin
of a cool, sweet
watermelon.

Green is money
to spend on
having a good time.

Red is the rose
that blooms
all summer long.

Red is a cheek
blushing from
the wind.

Red is the blood
running through
our veins.

Red is a valentine
sending thoughts
of love.

Pattern

Line 1: Color name is (noun)
Line 2: Beginning of a phrase describing noun
Line 3: End of the phrase describing the noun

What to do

1. Bring a bright-colored object to class: a flower, a balloon, a fruit, or just a large piece of colored paper. Ask the students to name the color and then to suggest different things associated with the color. Explain that people often describe a color by saying something is "as blue as the sky" or "as white as snow." As students suggest items associated with the color, write it in the pattern of "as _____ as _____ ." If students need help, you might suggest different categories such as

71

flowers, foods, or animals. Often students will name concrete nouns (e.g., for red, they might name a tomato, a clown's nose, lips, or a rose), but English idioms also suggest abstract nouns: green with envy, a blue mood, or tickled pink. Such phrases offer an opportunity to introduce either the idea of abstract nouns or idiomatic phrases having to do with colors.

2. Have students name other colors and identify associated concepts. Your list might end up like this:

> As gold as honey
> As blue as the sky
> As white as snow
> As red as a beet
> As green as grass

3. Select one color and get as many suggestions as possible for it. Write down the students' words associated with the color named. For instance, if the color is white, students may have suggested:

> snow   a swan
> a blank piece of paper   a lily
> a ghost   a wedding dress

4. Explain that students are going to write a poem with several verses based on a single color. Show a sample or two and have the students look for the pattern of the poem: each stanza a complete sentence naming the color, a noun, and a phrase or clause that describes the noun. Also explain that each verse is a separate metaphor, a figure of speech in which the noun they name represents the color.

5. Select three or four of the items named and ask students to help you write the three or four verses by describing the items selected. For instance, the list of white items might become:

> White is the snow
> covering the ground
> on a winter day.
>
> White is a blank piece of paper
> waiting for thoughts
> to become words.
>
> White is a lily
> floating gracefully
> on a pond.
>
> White is a ghost
> that haunts
> your scary dreams.

6. Divide the class into small groups and hand out a piece of colored paper to each group. Ask the students to brainstorm all the things associated with that color, select three or four, and write their own poem.
7. Have the students share their poems aloud.
8. Let students select their own colors and write their own poems.

Uses

- to introduce color names
- to introduce idiomatic expressions that include colors
- to introduce vocabulary associated with different colors (e.g., gray elephant, yellow sun, blue sky)

Student-written examples

Green
Green is a frog
jumping up and down.

Green is a leaf
falling from a tree.

Green is an alligator
waiting to eat.

Green is grass
growing from the ground.

Green is a turtle
swimming in the water.
—Elizabeth Gordon Taylor's
    class (ages 6 and 7)

Orange
Orange is a pumpkin
growing from a seed.

Orange is a fruit
waiting to be eaten.

Orange is a balloon
floating behind the clouds.

Orange is a salamander
crawling through the rain forest.

Orange is a snowman's nose
made from a carrot.

Orange is a tiger's fur,
soft, and striped.
—Elizabeth Gordon Taylor's
    class (ages 6 and 7)

White
White is paper
waiting for a pencil.

White is snow
falling from the sky.

White is polar bears
playing on the ice.

White is the clouds
floating in the sky.

White is a cat
playing with yarn.
—Elizabeth Gordon Taylor's
    class (ages 6 and 7)

Black
Black is the newt
swimming in a pond.

Black is the marker
writing on the board.

Black is the knight
riding his horse to the castle.

Black is the panther
lurking in the trees.
—Ian Vitanger (age 8),
    Chris Dazo (age 8)

Red
Red are the cells
of my blood
that flows in my body.

Red is the cardinal
that flies in the sky.

Red is a rose
that has lots of thorns.

Red are the cherries
that we eat in the spring.
—Abraham Rodriguez (age 8),
    Antonia Arias (age 8),
    Randy Aleman (age 8)

Pink
Pink is a pig
that rolls in the mud.

Pink is a rose
that a girl smells.

Pink is an eraser
that's on a pencil.

Pink are lips
that we use to kiss.
—Layla Medina (age 8),
    Silvia Montenegro (age 8),
    Xiomara Tejada (age 8)

Yellow
Yellow is the sun
shining in the sky.

Yellow is the sunflower
that makes the garden beautiful.

Yellow are the stars
that make the night light.

Yellow is the moon
watching over us.
—Eliza Hunanyan (age 12),
   Julio Pereyra (age 13),
   Yone Hailemarian (age 12)

Yellow
Yellow is the sun
shining on my face
early in the morning.

Yellow is a sunflower
growing in
my grandma's garden.

Yellow is a banana
waiting for me
to feel and eat.

Yellow is a canary
singing happily
in a tree.
—Joannie Monroy's class
   (ages 14 to 17)

Blue
Blue is the prince –
the one that I dream about.

Blue are his eyes
that drive me crazy.

Blue is the ocean
where my heart likes to swim.

Blue is the sky
where the rainbow ends.

Blue is the pen
that I use to write poems for him
that I never have the courage
      to give.
—Erika Merlos (age 13),
   Karen Montiel (age 13),
   Monica Alvarez (age 12)

Pink
Pink are the cherry blossoms
blooming
in my garden.

Pink is a strawberry ice-cream
      cone
that tastes good
on a hot summer's day.

Pink are my lips
forming
a happy smile.

Pink is a little baby girl
that gives joy
to her mom and dad.
–Cristina Paredes (age 15),
   Katy Martinez (age 15),
   Jose Alvarado (age 16)

Lesson 11

Gold

Gold are the fish
that swim
in the ocean.

Gold is the precious ring
that fits
on a bride's finger.

Gold is the sunshine
that wakes us
every morning.

Gold is the honey
that sweetens
our lives.
—Denise Hernandez (age 15),
  Leo Cejas (age 14),
  Bertha Hernandez (age 16),
  Elizabeth Caro (age 15)

White

White is the elephant
for the past Thai king.

White is religion
that teaches us
throughout our whole lives.

White is pure love
that people are looking for.

White is the American woman
whom I am falling in love with.

White is a star
shining in the sky.
—Namphol Puntuwongsa (adult)

Orange

Orange is flame
that toasts
my marshmallow.

Orange is a traffic light
that slows down
your car.

Orange is autumn leaves
that fall
here and there.

Orange is soda
that comes
with my combo meals.

Orange is fashion
like the trendiest boutique
where everything mismatches.

Orange is the sound of
        firecrackers
that warm me
all night long.

Orange is the sun
that burns me
on a summer day.

Orange is popcorn
that accompanies me
during the movie.

Orange is a sunset
that ends
my long day.
—Kris (Wahyu) Kristiyanto
  (adult)

Red
Red is temptation
that your moves invite.

Red is fire
that burns your love.

Red is a strawberry
that you share on your first date.

Red is chili
when your partner hates you.
—Mikyoung Lee, Kris (Wahyn) Kristiyanto,
   Juan Carlos Perlaza (adults)

12 Contrast poem

Teaching points: Simple and compound sentence structure
Linking verbs followed by adjectives
Verbs in the negative form
The conjunction *but*

The contrast poem allows students to practice the use of linking verbs followed by adjectives. Using complete sentences, students describe a given topic by linking descriptive characteristics to the topic. Generally, the poem is four lines, with the first three lines being similar characteristics or traits and the last line being an opposite characteristic or trait. The poem may be rhymed or unrhymed.

A dog is friendly.   Babies look cute.
A dog is intelligent.   Babies look sweet.
A dog is loyal,   Babies look funny,
but a dog isn't human.   but they don't look mean.

Flowers smell good.
Candy smells sweet.
Lemons smell fresh,
but none smells like feet!

Patterns

A ———— is ———— .
A ———— is ———— .
A ———— is ———— .
but a ———— is not ———— .

Subject ——(linking verb)—— adjective.
Subject ——(linking verb)—— adjective.
Subject ——(linking verb)—— adjective,
but subject ——(negative) (linking verb)—— adjective.

What to do

1. Bring in a picture or replica of something the class has been studying: a stuffed animal, a model of the solar system, a flower, or a leaf of a tree. Write the main idea on the board and place plus and minus signs at the top of two columns:

Snake characteristics

+   −

2. Ask the students to list the attributes or characteristics of the item. For example, for a snake students might say: "It has fangs," "It has a long, skinny tongue," "It is poisonous." Write the students' responses on the board under the plus sign, perhaps pointing out that some characteristics might be specific for one kind of snake but not for all snakes.

3. Ask the students for items that are *not* characteristic of the main idea. For example, for the snake, students might suggest: "Its real home is not a zoo," "It doesn't have a feet or legs," or "It doesn't make a good pet." Write the students' responses on the board under the minus sign. Some students tend to go far afield when suggesting noncharacteristics, so point out that the noncharacteristic item should fit logically within the main idea.

4. Show the students the pattern of the poem, pointing out how the first three lines are characteristics of the topic, but the last line is something that is not a characteristic. Also point out that the same verb is used in all four lines, so some rephrasing will be needed to create the poem from the students' original statements. You might also want to point out that each of the first two lines is a complete sentence, whereas the last two lines are a compound sentence (two independent clauses joined with a comma and a conjunction).

5. Have the students decide which characteristics to use to create the first three lines of the poem and which noncharacteristic should be used for the last line. Have them also decide what verb to use (*is, has, does,* etc.). Point out that some verbs (*doesn't*) take auxiliaries to form the negative (for example, *he has* becomes *he does not have*. The poem might evolve into:

A snake has fangs.
A snake has scales.
A snake has a forked tongue,
but a snake doesn't have legs.

6. Have the students work in small groups to create their own poems. If you have been studying particular animals, plants, or any other group of items, you might want to list topics from which students can

choose. If you are just beginning to study a particular group of items and resources on them are available, you might want to have students research their topics before writing their poems. Picture dictionaries may be helpful.

7. When the students have finished writing their poems, have them share their work by reading the poems aloud. They should now be ready to write their own poems.

Uses

• to analyze groups or classes of animals, plants, and inanimate objects by having students identify their characteristics (attributes) and noncharacteristics (nonattributes)
• to summarize a past event or story plot

Variations

1. The definition poem, excellent for teaching attributes and nonattributes as well as synonyms and antonyms, can be varied by changing the verb(s) in the stem(s). While the basic pattern uses linking verbs and encourages the use of adjectives, variations can include such stems as:

A _____ has _____ .
A _____ does _____ .
A _____ changes _____ .

Virtually any verb that allows for description will work:

A bicycle has two wheels.
A bicycle has a seat.
A bicycle has a set of brakes, but a bicycle has no feet.

Nature changes the seasons.
Nature changes the moon and sun.
Nature changes the butterflies and bees,
but she doesn't change the sheets.

2. Past-time verbs can be used in the stems so that students can describe stories of fiction or past events:

Cinderella had a cruel stepmother.
Cinderella had two ugly sisters.
Cinderella had a life of hard work,
but she was the one who married the prince.

I have forgotten the smell of book-pressed roses.
I have forgotten the lines of our high school pledge.
I have forgotten the names in the yearbook pages,
but I have never forgotten your soft brown eyes.

3. Rather than the same verb being repeated in each line, repeat an introductory phrase instead:

Last summer I enjoyed my time at the farm.
Last summer I swam in the lake.
Last summer I played with ponies in the field,
but I never took time to think.

Student-written examples

Candy
Candy is yummy.
Candy is colorful.
Candy is chocolate,
but candy is not pizza.
—Priscilla Palomino (age 7)

The elephant
An elephant has a trunk.
An elephant has big feet.
An elephant has floppy ears,
but an elephant doesn't have a
tiny body.
—Leslie Ramirez (age 8)

Pizza
A pizza has cheese.
A pizza has pepperoni.
A pizza has sauce,
but a pizza doesn't have pickles.
—Anthony Gonzalez (age 8)

The desert
A desert has snakes.
A desert has cacti.
A desert has sand,
but a desert doesn't have much
    water.
—Davis Martinez (age 8)

Big and small
A giraffe is big.
An elephant is big.
A dinosaur is big,
but a mouse is small.
—Jacklyn Tarin (age 13)

The zebra
A zebra has black and white stripes.
A zebra is a mammal from Africa.
A zebras runs fast like a horse,
But a zebra doesn't lay eggs.
—Claudette Willems's class
    (ages 14 to 17)

Lesson 12

The cloud
It wasn't an angel.
It wasn't spilled milk.
It wasn't a birthday cake.
It was just a cloud in the sky.
—Claudette Willems's class
    (ages 14 to 17)

Big Mac
Big Mac is big.
Big Mac is good.
Big Mac is cheap,
but it is not good for my diet.
—Lorena Barajas,
    Veronica Barajas (adults)

The clock
The clock helps me to go to work on time.
The clock helps me to know when to watch the movies.
The clock helps me to go to the doctor's early,
but the clock does not help me to be happy in the morning!
—Blas Armenta (adult)

Lipstick
Lipstick is red.
Lipstick is smooth.
Lipstick is expensive,
but it doesn't taste good.
—Marisela Flores (adult)

13 Countdown poem

Teaching points: Number words
Complete sentences
Logical sequence

The countdown poem is based on a numerical sequence. It can be based on a theme, as many counting books are, that describes objects, or it can tell a story, as the poem "Ten Little Indians" does. The sequence can be either forward or backward, depending on the students' creativity.

One bumble bee flew between
Two flowers, dropping
Three bits of pollen. He buzzed
Four times as he flew away. The next spring,
Five flowers grew where there had been only two.

One full moon glowed in the sky.
Two people watched it.
Three owls flew by it.
Four dogs howled at it.
And the moon just sat there.

Five fingers on my hand.
Four if you don't count my thumb.
Three of my fingers make a pledge.
Two of my fingers make a peace
     sign.
One of my fingers points the way.

Pattern

Line 1: One . . .
Line 2: Two . . .
Line 3: Three . . .
Line 4: Four . . .
Continue with as many numbers as desired.
Final line: Ending to the idea begun.

Note: Numbers can be counted backward.

Lesson 13

What to do

1. Show the students several sample poems and read them aloud. Ask students what they notice about the first word of each line in the poems (that each line starts with a number word). Point out that each one tells a little story about or describes a single subject. You might also point out the different structures that are possible for the lines: phrases, single sentence lines, and sentences that "wrap" around lines to make each line start with a number.

2. Have the students sit in a circle while you stand at the board. Tell them that they are going to create a countdown poem together. Ask them where they want to go (in their minds): school, the zoo, the park, the shopping mall, or a particular room in a house.

3. Once they decide, tell them that they're going to tell what they see there, but they're going to use numbers in order and then repeat what and how many of the object each one sees. For instance, if they decide to go to the zoo, one student might start by saying, "I saw one elephant." The next student would say, "I saw one elephant and two lions." The third student would say, "I saw one elephant, two lions, and three bears." Continue around the circle.

4. While the students are making up their additional sightings and repeating what the previous students have said, write their words on the board:

> We went to the zoo, where we saw
> One elephant
> Two lions
> Three bears . . .

Note: This works well with about fifteen students. With more students, either pair the students or take two different "trips."

5. When the students have all responded, tell them that they have the beginning of a countdown poem. Now they can add to each line by telling what each animal was doing. For example:

> We went to the zoo, where we saw
> One elephant washing himself with his trunk,
> Two lions roaring
> Three bears sleeping in their den . . .

6. Ask the students to think of a final line that sums up what they saw at the zoo, and add it to the poem:

> We went to the zoo, where we saw
> One elephant washing himself with his trunk,
> Two lions roaring
> Three bears sleeping in their den . . .
> It was a very busy day at the zoo.

7. Read the poem aloud to see if the lines fit together well or if more or less detail is needed.
8. Place the students in small groups to practice writing their own poems. To help them get started, you might want to assign a topic to each group. Some topics that have worked well with our students include:

a clothing store	a jewelry store	the beach
McDonald's	a picnic	a park
a car race	the grocery store	
the forest	a hospital	

9. Have students share their poems aloud. They should now be ready to write their own individual poems.

Uses

- to describe a content-related concept (the environment, the zoo, geometric figures)
- to tell a story in logical sequence

Student-written examples

The rainforest
One toucan sitting in the top of a tree,
Two harpy eagles hunting and feeding their young,
Three boa constrictors squeezing their prey,
Four monkeys howling and hanging on a vine,
Five jaguars searching for meat to eat,
Six lizards changing their colors for camouflage,
Seven leaf-cutter ants making food for their young,
Eight bats drinking nectar from flowers,
Nine hummingbirds flying to their nests,
Ten butterflies emerging from their chrysalides:
The rain-forest animals are a very busy group.
—Elizabeth Gordon Taylor's class (ages 6 and 7)

The sky
One moon shining in the sky
Two Milky Ways glowing in
    space
Three rings around Saturn
Four hot suns
Five stars shining like diamonds.
—Jasmine Espinoza (age 8)

Dinosaurs
One T. rex runs around
Two trees to catch
Three raptors but
Four pterodactyls got there
    first. Only
Five bones were left.
—Jose Ramirez (age 8),
    Davis Martinez (age 8)

The race
Five cars start the race.
Four cars crash.
Three cars are fixed in the race.
Two people are run over.
One person wins all the money.
—Edgar Martinez (age 12),
    Jose Soto (age 13),
    Alex Villalobos (age 11)

At the beach
One day my friend and I and
Two dogs went to the beach
    to play
Three games. We stayed
Four hours and bought
Five hamburgers because by
Six o'clock we were really
    hungry.
—Cesar Sosa (age 11),
    Elvisdiela Guzman (age 12),
    Luis De Oleo (age 11)

A picnic
Ten people went to a picnic at
Nine o'clock in the morning with
Eight sandwiches and
Seven sodas. They were looking for
Six chairs and
Five tables for their group, but they only found
Four. So,
Three people had to sit on the sand and
Two bugs bit them
One time!
—Sandra Gonzalez (age 14), Vanhdala Keomalavong (age 17),
    Linhnaphone Bouaravong (age 17)

Jewelry theft
One wicked pickpocket went to
    a jewelry store.
Two women were working
    behind the counter.
Three cameras were in the store.
Four witnesses were shopping.
Five diamonds were stolen.
Six rubies disappeared. Then
Seven minutes later the police
    came.
Eight policemen entered and
    arrested the wicked
    pickpocket.
—Eduardo Campos (age 16),
    Jose Gomez (age 15),
    Juan Jurado (age 16)

The car garage
One day I went to the car garage
    because I had
Two flat tires. I paid
Three dollars for each repair.
Four hours later, I got my car
    back.
Five days later, the tires were
    flat again.
Oh my God!
—Jose Lomeli, Luis Garcia
    (adults)

At the mall
One day
Two people went to the mall to buy
Three pairs of pants,
Four T-shirts, and
Five pairs of shoes.
They went home broke.
—Claudette Willems's class (ages 14 to 17)

Clothing store
One day I went to "Fashion Q"
    with my
Two sisters. We looked at
Three different kinds of
    clothing and
Four pairs of shoes. We stayed
    there for
Five hours trying on all the
    clothes and
Six hours later, we didn't buy
    anything.
Seven hours later, we had a
    terrible headache!
—Lorena Barajas,
    Veronica Barajas (adults)

On the freeway
One morning I was going down
    the freeway.
Two cars went by very fast.
Three persons were in each car.
Four police cars followed the
    two cars.
Five accidents happened along
    the way.
Six persons were injured and
Seven reporters took the news.
—Araceli Villanueva,
    Marisela Flores (adults)

14 Days-of-the-week poem

Teaching points: Punctuation and capitalization of proper nouns
Days of the week (sequence and spelling)
Paragraphing concepts: unity and coherence
Sensory verbs

By telling a brief story using days of the weeks as the sequencing vehicle, students learn the order and spelling of those words. They also learn rudimentary elements of paragraphing in that each sentence in their story must relate to the chosen theme.

At the beach
On Monday I saw the ocean.
On Tuesday I touched the sand.
On Wednesday I heard the waves.
On Thursday I tasted the salt in
    the air.
On Friday I smelled the moist
    sea breeze.
On Saturday I felt the cool blue water.
On Sunday I heard the seagulls.

My new puppy
On Monday I saw my new puppy.
On Tuesday I touched her fur.
On Wednesday I heard her barking.
On Thursday I smelled her breath.
On Friday I tasted her love.

Pattern

On Monday I saw _____ .
On Tuesday I touched _____ .
On Wednesday I heard _____ .
On Thursday I tasted _____ .
On Friday I smelled _____ .
On Saturday I (sensory verb) _____ .
On Sunday I (any verb) _____ .

Note: The last two lines are optional. Verbs may be sequenced in any logical order.

What to do

1. Design and copy a 1-week calendar with boxes for each day of the week written at the top. Or ask students to divide a sheet of notebook paper into 5 to 7 sections and write the days of the week at the top of each section. Model the calendar on the board or overhead projector, filling in the days of the week as the students recite and spell them.

2. Discuss sensory verbs (*heard, saw, tasted, smelled, touched*) and ask students to write one sensory verb in each box of their weekly calendar. Model this on the 1-week calendar on the board.

3. Explain to the students that they will be writing a poem that uses the days of the week and these verbs. Show them some sample poems and ask them what they notice about the first two words of each line ("On Monday," "On Tuesday," etc.). Then ask them what the verb is in each line so that they are aware that sensory verbs are the main verbs for this poem.

4. Select a topic to use as a model. Write the topic at the top of the 1-week calendar. Model the pattern of the sentence by writing "On Monday I (heard, saw, tasted, smelled, or touched)" and ask the students to help you write the rest of the sentence to fit your topic. For instance, if you chose the week before Christmas as your topic, you might begin by asking students what you might see the week before Christmas. The line might become:

On Monday I saw Santa Claus at the mall.

5. Continue with the other days and verbs to create a 5-day poem. The poem might continue:

On Monday I saw Santa Claus at the mall.
On Tuesday I smelled the Christmas tree.
On Wednesday I heard sleigh bells ringing.
On Thursday I tasted cookies and hot chocolate.
On Friday I touched the gifts of the season.

6. Divide students into groups and have them fill in their days-of-the-week boxes with sensory experiences from a topic of their choosing. If students have difficulty selecting, you might provide suggestions on cards. Some ideas we have used include:

a perfect (ideal) week   a week of winter vacation
a week in my school life   a week of spring break
a week during a holiday   a week of vacation in a special place
a week of summer vacation

7. Have students transpose the information from the calendar boxes into a linear poem as presented in the model.

8. Ask students to read their poems aloud within their groups and to rearrange sentences to tell a better story. Have them add detail (adjectives, adverbs, etc.) where they can to better express their experiences.

Uses

- to tell a story in sequence
- to recount a historical event
- to describe a holiday, event, place, etc.

Variations

1. Although the days-of-the-week model uses sensory verbs in the past tense to tell a story, any other verbs or tenses might also be used with equal effect. For example:

On Monday I will tell her I love her.
On Tuesday I will buy her a ring.
On Wednesday I will ask for her hand.
On Thursday I will kneel at her feet.
On Friday I will hear her answer.

On Monday I crammed for a biology exam.
On Tuesday I took the big test.
On Wednesday I worried about my grade.
On Thursday I found out I'd passed.
On Friday I celebrated my success.

2. Months of the year can be substituted for days of the week. This variation encourages students to associate seasons and holidays with various months. For example:

In January I studied Martin Luther King.
In February I got Valentines.
In March my parents took me to the beach for spring break.
In April I counted tulips.

3. The beginning of each line can be changed to describe almost any sequence such as seasons (spring, summer, autumn, winter), parts of the day (morning, afternoon, evening, night), times (six o'clock, seven o'clock, eight o'clock, etc.), or ages (ten, twenty, thirty, etc.):

In spring I sniffed the daffodils.
In summer I played with my friends.
In autumn I helped rake leaves.
In winter I shoveled the snow.

By seven o'clock I was out of bed.
By nine o'clock I was in my seat at school.
By eleven o'clock I was really hungry.
By one o'clock I was full from lunch.
By three o'clock I was ready to go home.
By five o'clock I was hungry again.
By nine o'clock I was back in bed again.

4. In any of the models, verb tenses may also be mixed to show a progression from the past to the future.

Student-written examples

Winter
On Monday I saw snow falling.
On Tuesday I touched a snowman.
On Wednesday I heard the blowing wind.
On Thursday I tasted gingerbread cookies.
On Friday I smelled hot chocolate.
On Saturday I heard the jingle bells of Santa's sleigh.
On Sunday I felt wonderful!
—Elizabeth Gordon Taylor's class (ages 6 and 7)

On the farm
On Monday we smell a henhouse.
On Tuesday we see pigs rolling in the mud.
On Wednesday we touch a horse.
On Thursday we taste chicken.
On Friday we hear roosters singing.
—Antonio Arias (age 8), Davis Martinez (age 8),
   Abraham Rodriguez (age 8)

First date
On Monday I saw a boy.
On Tuesday I heard his name.
On Wednesday I touched his hand.
On Thursday I tasted chocolate.
On Friday I smelled roses.
On Saturday we went on a date.
—Viridiana Trujillo (age 11)

At Grandma's house
On Monday I saw my grandma.
On Tuesday I touched her hand.
On Wednesday I heard the TV show with her.
On Thursday I tasted her apple pie.
On Friday I smelled the flowers I gave her.
—Aileen Ruiz (age 13)

Día de la bandera
On Monday I heard *el Presidente.*
On Tuesday I touched *la bandera.*
On Wednesday I tasted the red hot *tamales.*
On Thursday I heard the *mañanitas.*
On Friday I saw the parade for the Mexican flag.
—Juan Carlos Reyes (age 15),
    Arturo Caro (age 16),
    Luz Yadira Melendez (age 16)

A Washington week
On Monday I saw the White House.
On Tuesday I heard the President speak.
On Wednesday I touched his hand.
On Thursday I smelled the cherry blossoms.
On Friday I tasted the success of my trip.
On Saturday I watched the video of my trip.
On Sunday I was ready for the next day of school.
—Gerson Huertero (age 15),
    Phoubeck Sithovong (age 16),
    Maria Arcos (age 15)

A week in my school life
On Monday we saw our best friends.
On Tuesday we smelled the food in the cafeteria.
On Wednesday we heard the teacher's voice.
On Thursday we tasted a big pepperoni pizza.
On Friday we went to assembly.
On Saturday we slept until 9 o'clock.
On Sunday we did our homework.
—Jhoselyn Alfaro (age 15), Marcos Martinez (age 16),
    Anneck Sithovong (age 17)

Girlfriend
On Monday I saw the sun in your window.
On Tuesday I touched the cool water in your shower.
On Wednesday I heard the song of the happy birds in your trees.
On Thursday I tasted the sweet menthol of your lips.
On Friday I smelled the flowers in your heart.
—Luis Garcia (adult)

New girl
On Monday I saw a new girl in class.
On Tuesday I touched her fine hands.
On Wednesday I heard her angelic laughing.
On Thursday I smelled her beautiful perfume.
On Friday I tasted her soft, red lips.
—Francisco Villa Maldonado (adult)

My backyard
On Monday I saw my backyard after work.
On Tuesday I touched the plants and the roses.
On Wednesday I heard the birds in my trees.
On Thursday I tasted the first orange from my trees.
On Friday I smelled the flowers and fruit plants.
—Blas Armenta (adult)

Mexico City
On Monday I saw the colonial buildings in the town.
On Tuesday I touched the Mexican arts and adornments.
On Wednesday I heard the Mariachi in Garibaldi.
On Thursday I tasted delicious Mexican food.
On Friday I smelled the smog of many cars.
—Alma Castillo (adult)

15 Diamante

Teaching points: Synonyms and antonyms (use of a thesaurus)
Adjectives
Participles
Thesis-antithesis

The diamante, like the cinquain, is useful for teaching parts of speech: nouns, adjectives, and participial phrases. The diamante can be more challenging, however, in that it is based on either thesis-antithesis or metamorphosis. Students must be able to understand and describe opposite concepts or concepts that change over time. Because the poem is constructed from opposite ends almost at the same time, it can introduce students to the idea of nonlinear sequencing, that is, the idea that not every piece of writing is constructed from beginning to end in a sequential order.

Black

Dark, scary

Hiding, shading, closing

Witches, night – angels, day

Shining, brightening, opening

Light, happy

White

Love

Happy, sweet

Energizing, satisfying, sacrificing

Flame, admiration – hostility, iciness

Draining, loathing, self-serving

Violent, sad

Hate

Pattern

Line 1: One noun
Line 2: Two adjectives related to the first noun
Line 3: Three participles (*-ing, -ed*) related to the first noun
Line 4: Four nouns, two related to the first noun and two related to the second
Line 5: Three participles (*-ing, -ed*) related to the second noun
Line 6: Two adjectives related to the second noun
Line 7: One noun (antithesis or metamorphosis of the first noun)

What to do

1. Explain to students that the poem they are going to write is called a diamante because it's shaped like a diamond. Show them some samples and draw a diamond shape around one of the samples to highlight the form.

2. After reading the samples aloud, ask the students to identify the pattern by naming the parts of speech in each line and counting how many of each are in the line. Point out how the parts of speech and the numbers of words in each line create a mirror image; that is, the first and last lines are both single nouns, the second and sixth lines are each two adjectives, and so on.

3. Ask the students to identify the difference in meaning between the first and last lines, the second and sixth lines, and so on. They should notice that the first and last lines are either antonyms (love/hate) or an evolution from one thing to another (rain/flood). You may want to have them think of the poem as a kind of dialogue between two people who disagree totally but who find a connection somewhere in the middle.

4. Explain that to write this poem and create the diamond shape, they will begin from both the top and the bottom and finish in the middle.

5. Ask students to think of pairs of nouns that are opposites, writing the words on the board as they suggest them. After students have generated many pairs, you may want to have them note which pairs of nouns are concrete and which are abstract.

6. Have students select a pair of nouns that interests them. Write the first noun of the pair centered at the top of the board and the second noun centered at the bottom.

7. Ask students to think of adjectives that relate to each noun. Make two lists on the board as students suggest words. If students have difficulty thinking of opposing adjectives, encourage them to use a thesaurus. Ask students to select from their lists two adjectives that describe the first noun and two that describe the second noun. Place the first two adjectives on line 2, centered under the first noun. Place the adjectives that describe the second noun on line 6, centered above the second noun. Demonstrate the use of commas to separate the two adjectives.

8. For the present participles in lines 3 and 5, follow the same brainstorming and selection process used with the adjectives. As you transfer the participles to the board, demonstrate the use of commas to separate items in a series. Place the participles describing the first noun centered on line 3, and the participles describing the second noun centered on line 5.

9. For the final line of the poem, line 4, ask students to think of other

nouns that relate to the nouns chosen for lines 1 and 7. Select two nouns that most aptly extend the definition of the first word of the poem and place those two words on line 4. Then select two nouns which describe the last word of the poem and place those words also on line 4. Demonstrate the use of commas to separate words and the use of a dash to separate the opposite concepts. If single nouns do not work well for the antonyms used, you may want to vary the pattern to noun phrases to make it easier. For instance, in a class working with the idea of dogs versus cats, the students came up with "pack animal – solitary predator" for this middle line.

10. Read the poem aloud, asking students if they wish to change or alter the poem in any way to more accurately reflect their thinking or their sense of rhythm and balance.

11. Divide the students into small groups to write their own diamantes. If they have difficulty selecting a topic, you may want to hand out topics to get them started. Some topics we have used include:

sun/moon	ice/water
sky/earth	angel/devil
mother/father	Cinderella/stepsisters
summer/winter	Snow White/witch
dogs/cats	Clark Kent/Superman

Uses

- to develop abstract thinking (e.g., freedom versus slavery, love versus hate)
- to describe natural phenomena that are opposites (e.g., acids versus bases, sun versus moon, liquids versus solids)
- to describe protagonists and antagonists
- to describe friends, family, or pets that differ significantly
- to describe a change or metamorphosis (rain into flood, Cinderella into princess, tadpole into frog)
- to describe a person (first name/last name for first/last lines)

Student-written examples

Windy
Little, great
Fishing, writing, playing
Girl, daughter – sister, friend
Trying, drawing, singing
Playful, learned
Wong
—Windy Wong (age 7)

Caterpillar
Chubby, fat
Spinning, chewing, crawling
Growing insect – awaking
beauty
Flapping, flying, soaring
Winged, pretty
Butterfly
—Betsy Anguiana (age 9),
Roxana Cano (age 9)

Winter
Cold, wet
Snowing, shivering, freezing
White, gray – yellow, orange
Blazing, sweating, roasting
Hot, sunny
Summer
—Jennifer Villatoro (age 9)

Sun
Yellow, round
Glistening, sparkling, shining
Hot day – cool evening
Glowing, floating, changing
White, crescent
Moon
—Amy Moreno (age 9),
Pairisblu Davis (age 9)

Girls
Crazy, *amable*
Talking, making-up, flirting
Young women – young men
Playing, swearing, shouting
Macho, cute
Boys
—Luis Marin (age 12),
Daniel Felix (age 13),
Maria Hernandez (age 13)

Dione Sanders
Quick, buff
Running, shaking, catching
Football hero – basketball hero
Jumping, dunking, dribbling
Tall, thin
Michael Jordan
—Philmon Girmay (age 11),
Milan Kodic (age 13),
Gerardo Novoa (age 13)

Circle
Round, smooth,
Rolling, bouncing, scoring
Sphere, ball – quadrilateral, box
Cubed, hollowed, sitting
Flat, sharp
Square.
—Deonoveigh Mitchell (age 13)

Brother
Handsome, athlete
Walking, running, playing
Gym, sport – makeup, mall
Shopping, talking, singing
Beautiful, intelligent
Sister
—Evelyn Jaime (age 11)

Cinderella
Beautiful, poor
Cleaning, singing, crying
Kind princess – mean siblings
Fighting, screaming, dressing
Ugly, lazy
Stepsisters
—Daisy Camarena (age 15),
Linhnaphone Bouaravong
(age 17), Vanhdala
Keomalavong (age 17),
Rocio Mora (age 16)

Angel
Kind, helpful
Loving, aiding, saving
Good spirit – bad spirit
Hating, tempting, taking
Evil, scary
Devil
—Marizol Cisneros (age 17),
Juan Jurado (age 16),
Jose Gomez (age 15)

Teacher
Mature, smart
Teaching, talking, standing
Scholar, graduate – pupil, undergraduate
Learning, listening, sitting
Immature, young
Student
– Lien Dang (adult)

Police
Good, smart
Catching, caring, helping
Station, gun – gun, prison
Stealing, running, hiding
Bad, mean
Thief
– Yoshi Takemura (adult)

16 Five senses poem

Teaching points: Sensory verbs
Basic sentence structure
Metaphors and similes
Phrases

The five senses poem is useful for teaching basic sentence structure, but it can be expanded to create more complex patterns. Each line of the poem (except for the first) creates a simile to which students can add descriptive details, participial phrases, and relative clauses.

Vacation is grass green and sunshine yellow.
It tastes like strawberry ice cream dripping down your chin.
It sounds like the gentle waves of the ocean.
It smells like the coconut oil in suntan lotion.
It looks like the glare of the sun shining on the sand.
It makes me feel like a big, red beach ball.

Pattern

Line 1: (An emotion or idea) is (one or two colors).
Line 2: It tastes like . . .
Line 3: It sounds like . . .
Line 4: It smells like . . .
Line 5: It looks like . . .
Line 6: It makes me feel (like) . . .

What to do

1. Be prepared with two or three topics that students will have feelings about. Depending on the school schedule, you may want to use a holiday or season (Halloween, Christmas, winter, spring). Special school events (e.g., dances and final exams) and sports activities also work well. Have the students select one topic to work on as a whole group.

2. Ask students for colors that they associate with the topic and have them select two as a group. For instance, Halloween might inspire *orange* and *black,* whereas spring might elicit *green* and *yellow.* Write the colors on the board.

3. Ask the students for adjectives that help describe each color. For instance, the Halloween example might inspire *pumpkin orange* and *midnight black,* whereas the spring example might evoke *grassy green* and *sunshine yellow.* On the chalkboard, write the line that has just been created (e.g., "Halloween is pumpkin orange and midnight black" or "Spring is grassy green and sunshine yellow").

4. Tell the students that they are going to write a poem starting with the line they have already created. Show them several sample poems and read them aloud. Then ask the students to look for a pattern in the lines of the poems. Go through each line until the students have discovered the pattern. Write the pattern on the board underneath the first line that the group has already written:

> It tastes like . . .
> It sounds like . . .
> It smells like . . .
> It looks like . . .
> It makes me feel . . .

5. Divide the class into five groups. Assign the second line of the poem to one group, the third line to another, the fourth line to another, and so on. Give the groups 3 to 5 minutes to write their assigned lines. At the end of the time allotted, have a spokesperson from each group read the line they created as you record it on the board.

6. Now read the entire poem aloud. In just a few minutes, the class has created a poem. *Note:* Although we have found that the lines created separately usually work well together, sometimes editing is needed: Repeated words may need synonyms. One group's view may have differed from the original idea. Or an uneven rhythm may need one less or one more word or syllable. Tell the students that each line by itself is good, but sometimes when things get pieced together the pieces don't always work as a whole. Ask the students if the ideas flow together well, if the rhythm sounds good to them, or if they have suggestions for word changes that might improve the poem.

7. Students should now be ready to begin writing their own poems as individuals, in pairs, or in small groups as the student samples illustrate.

Uses

- to clarify understanding of a season, food, or other content-related concept or idea
- to describe a concept in the student's native language that may defy direct translation
- to teach/learn similes inductively

Student-written examples

Basketball
Basketball is orange with black stripes.
It tastes like sweaty air.
It sounds like the whole crowd cheering for me.
It smells like dirty uniforms and sweaty shoes.
It looks like me shooting a three-point swish.
It makes me feel like a champion!
—Jorge Orozco (age 9), Ken Alexander (age 9)

The desert
The desert is red and yellow.
It tastes like a hot chili pepper.
It sounds like snakes rattling their tails.
It smells like the burning sun.
It looks like red rocks and dull sand.
It makes us feel hot and thirsty.
—Karmina Arreola (age 9), Natalie Perez (age 9)

Fire
Fire is red and orange.
It tastes like burning chili.
It sounds like kids jumping up and down on the bed.
It smells like death.
It looks like it's attacking people.
It makes me feel scared and hot.
—Bertha Salcido (age 9)

The ocean
The ocean is a dark blue color.
It tastes like salty cookies with homemade bread.
It sounds like seagulls laughing and mighty waves roaring.
It smells like newborn fish and fresh air.
It looks like a big, old blanket covering its sons and daughters.
It makes me feel welcome to swim in its fresh water.
—Xochitl Nava (age 9)

Soccer games
Soccer games are black and white because you start clean and you
    end dirty.
They taste like dry mouth.
They sound like bombs exploding.
They smell like sweat and dust.
They look like crazy people running around.
They make me feel excited.
—Gerardo Novoa (age 13), Milan Kodic (age 13)

My grandmother's kitchen
My grandmother's kitchen is shiny as a silver spoon.
It tastes like warm bread and homemade apple pie.
It sounds like drums playing as she kneads the dough.
It smells like early spring when spices are growing.
It looks like bright sunshine in the morning.
It makes me feel like having a party.
—Monica Patel (age 16), Cesar Gonzalez (age 16),
    PeeJay Tagudin (age 16), Falguni Patel (age 16)

'N Sync
'N Sync are baby blue.
They taste like sweet sugar.
They sound like loud pop.
They smell like good perfume.
They look like cute boys.
They make me feel like dancing.
—Eliza Hunanyan (age 12), Benyam Hailemariam (age 13),
    Julio Pereyra (age 13), Yone Hailemariam (age 12)

Chicas Latinas
Chicas Latinas are brown and tan like a mango.
They taste like banana splits on a hot summer day.
They sound like a tuba.
They smell like a garden of roses.
They look like a guitar with lots of beautiful *curvas.*
They make us feel like we're in heaven when they treat us good!
—Ricardo Bermudez (age 16), Rafael Peña (age 16),
    Jose Alvarado (age 16), Moses Araujo (age 16)

Final exam week

Final exam week is black like our minds and white like the paper
   we have to write on.
It tastes like a sour candy melting in your mouth.
It sounds like our knees hitting themselves together.
It smells like sweating hands writing over the test.
It looks like the last day of our lives.
It makes us feel like exploding air out of our heads.
—Elizabeth Caro (age 15), Francisco Tlatelpa (age 14),
   Bertha Hernandez (age 15), Leonardo Cejas (age 14)

Chocolate

Chocolate is golden brown and white.
It tastes like the first kiss that makes you want more.
It sounds like crunchy, dry leaves falling on the ground.
It smells like a warm memory from my childhood.
It looks like the best treasure, a big smile of a small child.
It makes me feel like floating on a cloud high over the earth!
—Marlene Onate, Mosammat Khanom, Unyoung Son,
   Kat Zdeb Toczynska, Marta Oliveira, Susana Gonzalez,
   Emi Sugiyama, Kyung Joon Kim (adults)

Jealousy

Jealousy is green and black.
It tastes like dust and old photos decaying.
It sounds like his voice calling in the night.
It smells like acid and sour milk mixed together.
It looks like frowns and sad smiles.
It makes me feel like sleeping with the blanket over my head.
—Marlene Onate, Mosammat Khanom, Unyoung Son,
   Kat Zdeb Toczynska, Marta Oliveira, Susana Gonzalez,
   Emi Sugiyama, Kyung Joon Kim (adults)

Money

Money is green and gold.
It tastes like caviar and champagne being drunk on the French Riviera.
It sounds like rock music hurting your ears and classical music
   comforting your mind.
It smells like a powerful, magnetic, night queen flower.
It looks like a drug; the more you get, the more you want.
It makes me feel like a dog with a big pile of bones; I want to guard
   it forever.
—Marlene Onate, Mosammat Khanom, Unyoung Son,
   Kat Zdeb Toczynska, Marta Oliveira, Susana Gonzalez,
   Emi Sugiyama, Kyung Joon Kim (adults)

17 Haiku

Teaching points: Syllabication
Spelling
Imagery
Conciseness of expression

Haiku is a kind of Japanese poetry that paints a picture of nature. It has a very controlled pattern of three lines containing seventeen syllables. For many students, knowledge of syllabication can lead to improved spelling.

Brown coconuts hang	At dawn, the sun's bright
From green palm trees, hiding like	Song shines out loud greetings as
A secret treasure.	It strikes trees and sky.

Pattern

Line 1: Five syllables
Line 2: Seven syllables
Line 3: Five syllables

What to do

1. Explain syllabication by taking a familiar poem or song and showing students how their chins drop each time a new syllable in the poem or song is pronounced. Have students place their hands beneath their chins to feel the drop as they repeat the syllables.
2. Reinforce their understanding of syllabication by having them tap on their desks or clap their hands as each syllable is pronounced. You might also want to point out that syllables may be deciphered visually based on one vowel sound (though it may be two or more actual vowel letters) per syllable.
3. Show the students samples of haiku and have them count the syllables for each line to practice their understanding of syllabication and to discover the pattern.

4. To point out that haiku creates a single, visual image of nature, have students select one of the haiku shown and draw a picture based on it.

5. Have students draw their own pictures or find pictures in magazines and art books that they would like to describe. Or take students outside to find an inspiration for their poems.

6. Model how you might proceed to create a haiku by using a picture of your own. For instance, looking at an enlarged picture of rain falling on flowers might lead you to think of words and phrases such as *pink flowers against a background of green leaves, rain pelting the flowers, the drops look like needles, some flowers droop from the rain's weight, other flowers look like they are opening up mouths to catch the rain, and the sun peeks shyly through the rain.*

7. Explain that you want to create a single image and, therefore, will take the one that has the flowers opening up to catch the rain. Perhaps you start with something like this:

> Pink petals open
> Their thirsty mouths wide
> To catch the rain.

As you and the students count the syllables, you'll notice that there are five in the first line but only five in the second and four in the third. Have students help you add words, rearrange words, and substitute words to follow the pattern needed. You might end up with something like this:

> Pink petals open
> Thirsty mouths wide to drink deeply
> From fast-falling rain.

Or perhaps, like this:

> Open pink petals,
> Thirsty mouths drinking deeply
> Through needles of rain.

8. Have students create their own haiku, getting help from each other for counting syllables and revising to fit the pattern and create a single picture.

Uses

- to describe topics in content areas such as science, geography, history, and math
- to summarize a book or story's setting
- to create a self-portrait or character sketch

- to complement an art lesson as the caption to a picture
- to reinforce students' ability to interpret the natural world

Student-written examples

Red hot lava spouts.
Volcanoes erupting ash,
Burning and melting.
—Noemi Torres (age 8)

From clouds emerges
A curving yellow rainbow
Disappearing fast.
—Jose Ramirez (age 8)

Prairie dog exits
From dark underground tunnel,
Sniffing for his food.
—Abraham Rodriguez
   (age 8)

Red butterflies fly
High up in the bright blue sky
Looking down on trees.
—Antonio Arias (age 8),
   Davis Martinez (age 8)

A moonlit night sky
Glows above the old cactus.
Sharp spines stay alert.
—Jasmine Espinoza (age 8)

Rain falls on green leaves
Birds hide under safe shelter
Until sun rises.
—Gemma Andaya (age 8)

Fall colors reflect
Mirrors of nature's beauty –
Peaceful crisp weather.
—Cecilia Arevalo (age 11)

Rainbow cuts through clouds.
Golden sunlight shines bright to
Wake up all the land.
—Ilay Ferrin (age 13)

Rainbow in the dusk
Peaceful river flowing slow
Mountains watching all.
—Mersad Zenelji (age 13)

Red tulips curtsey
Open their petals at dawn
Perfume so, so sweet.
—Linhnaphone Bouravong
   (age 17), Sandra Gonzalez (age
   14), Vanhdala Keomalavong
   (age 17)

Islands in the sea
Reflecting the soft rainbow
From high in the sky.
–Oscar Miranda (age 16),
   Oscar Morales (age 17),
   Mariano Alba (age 15)

The small hummingbird
Dips his long beak into pink
Trumpets to drink deep.
—Daisy Camarena (age 15),
   Marisol Cisneros (age 17),
   Rocio Mora (age 16)

Tulips and daisies
Standing like tall, strong soldiers
In our Freedom Park.
—Hina Patel (age 15), Chung Un Pak (age 17),
   Areli Ramirez (age 15), Sujin Lee (age 15)

Crystal turquoise sea
Joins the shore and granite rocks
Heaven's pleasure place.
—Mosammat Khanom, Susana Gonzalez (adults)

Pretty little bird
Sweet humming in my warm heart
Like a jeweled queen
—Emi Sugiyama (adult)

Quiet horizon
Peaceful on the river of
Innocent fisher.
—Mikyoung Lee, Jessica Munguia (adults)

18 Hero poem

Teaching points: Proper nouns, capitalization
Adjectives
Noun phrases
Prepositional phrases

The hero poem describes someone the writer admires by briefly telling why he or she is a hero. The hero is usually a real or fictional person, but animals may be heroes as well. Because the poem is based on the writer's thoughts, images, and feelings associated with the hero, it can give insight into the writer's interests and aspirations.

Big bird	Robin Williams
Huge, yellow, fluffy	Creative, zany, energetic
Friend to children	Comedian
Dancing, singing, entertaining	Analyzing, dissecting, satirizing
Every day on Sesame Street	On stage and in films
He's more than a bird – he's my buddy.	He knocks my socks off.

Pattern

Line 1: The name of a person (or other creature) you admire
Line 2: Three adjectives to describe that person
Line 3: Place, group, or activity identified with the person
Line 4: Three action words (-*ing* words) for the person
Line 5: When or where the person's actions take place
Line 6: Thoughts or feelings about the person

What to do

1. Depending on the time of year or the unit that you are studying in social studies, reading, or science, you might want to limit the parameters for choosing a hero to write about for this whole-class demonstration. Within those parameters, ask the students to choose a person or character that they believe is a good model for them to write about.

2. Write the chosen name centered at the top of the board. Point out the use of capital letters to distinguish proper nouns.

3. Show samples of the poem and ask students to identify the pattern based on the content and parts of speech in each line.

4. Ask the students to think of adjectives that describe the hero. Encourage students to generate many words, creating a word list from which they will choose only three to add to line 2 of the poem. Write the selected adjectives beneath the hero's name, demonstrating the use of commas to separate items in a series.

5. Have students discuss and decide on a place, group, or activity that is identified with the hero. Since this line may take the form of a noun phrase or a verb phrase, you might want to discuss the elements inherent to those phrases. Write the selected phrase on line 3 of the poem.

6. Ask students to generate a list of present participles (action words ending in – *ing*) that they associate with the hero. Have them select three from among their list and write them on line 4 of the poem, again demonstrating the use of commas to separate items in a series.

7. Since the next line generally takes the form of a prepositional phrase, you may want to model prepositional phrases by asking the students to tell you when or where the actions they described in line 4 take place. Write the phrase they create on line 5.

8. Ask students to dictate their feelings or thoughts about the hero in any form they wish. Write them on the board for the students to select one. This line can be either a phrase or a complete sentence, so it presents a good opportunity to teach the difference between complete sentences and phrases. Write the phrase or sentence in the final line of the poem.

9. Read the entire poem aloud. Ask students whether the separate lines flow together to create a cohesive image of the hero. If the poem does not cohere, ask for suggested revisions.

10. Students are now ready to select their own heroes and write their poems in small groups, in pairs, or as individuals.

Uses

- to describe a character from a book or story
- to describe a historical figure
- to depict figures associated with specific holidays (Easter bunny, Halloween goblins, and so on)
- to express admiration for someone looked up to
- to personify a science concept, a famous or historical site, or a natural phenomenon

Student-written examples

Kermit the frog
Green, funny, happy
Actor
Speaking, thinking, dancing
On television
We think he's wonderful!
—Elizabeth Gordon Taylor's
    class (ages 6 and 7)

Pencil,
Bright, yellow, sparkly,
It helps me write.
Scribbling, erasing, sharpening,
In my hand.
It gives me power on the paper.
—Bertha Salcido (age 9)

Luis Hernandez
Fast, smart, athletic
Great soccer player
Blocking, scoring, winning
On the Mexican national team
I would like to be like him.
—Irai Hernandez (age 9)

Selena
Pretty, nice, talented
Tex-Mex singer
Singing, dancing, entertaining
Around the world
How sad that she was killed.
—Jacqueline Garcia (age 11)

The Rock
Rough, mean, tough
The people's champ
Fighting, hitting, kicking
In the World Wrestling
    Federation
I like it when he does the rock
    bottom.
—Ken Alexander (age 9)

Jennifer
Brown-eyed, brown-haired,
    brown-skinned
She helps me, plays with me,
    makes me feel better
Hardworking, smiling, sharing
At school
She's a good friend.
—Abella Rutahindurwa (age 9)

The Beatles
Famous, young, smart
They started a new kind of
    music
Singing, playing guitars
composing songs
In London
They wrote my favorite song,
    "The Yellow Submarine."
—Lucero Rodriguez (age 9)

Gokou
Strong, powerful, yellow-haired
Japanese cartoon character
Sayaying, spirit-bombing,
    defending
Throughout the galaxy
He fights for good over evil.
—Lance Egan's class
    (ages 11 to 13)

Michael Jordan
Tall, rich, athletic
Basketball star for the Chicago Bulls
Dribbling, jumping, shooting
On the court
He is the best basketball player ever.
—Claudette Willems's class (ages 14 to 17)

Julia Roberts
Slim, beautiful, long-legged, talented
My Best Friend's Wedding
Acting, hard-working, smiling
In Hollywood
She is famous, open-minded, and sexy.
—Yelena Moore, Alina Radchenko,
    Konrad Sychowicz, Yumiko Tateno (adults)

Batman
Very quick, intelligent, bat-like
Flying, driving his batmobile, hanging out
With his loyal friend Robin
In Gotham City at night
He helps those in need.
—Claudette Willems's class (ages 14 to 17)

Jack-o'-lantern
Ugly, weird, scary
On Halloween day
Laughing, glowing, intimidating
In every house
Helps celebrate the scariest of days – Halloween.
—Daniel Shin, Jorge Morteo (adults)

19 "I am" poem

Teaching points: Sentences
Subordinate clauses
Relative clauses
Metaphors

The "I am" poem is a very personal poem that can help students explore their interests, dreams, fears, culture, and concerns. Since each line is a complete sentence, students must have an understanding of the basic sentence. The poem may also help students gain knowledge of subordinating and relative clauses to add more depth to their expression.

I am a studious girl who loves to read.
I wonder if I could someday be an author, too.
I hear the voices of characters talking as I read.
I see what they look like and what they are doing.
I want to be able to create my own stories and have other people
    read them.
I am a studious girl who loves to read.

I pretend that I am a character in a book.
I feel what she feels.
I touch the people she touches.
I worry that I won't be able to bring my characters to life.
I cry when I think my eyes won't be able to see the printed page
    some day.
I am a studious girl who loves to read.

I understand that I may not be a successful writer.
I say that success is in me and I must pursue it.
I dream of the joy my writing could bring to others.
I try to keep reading and writing to learn to do both better.
I hope my dream can come true.
I am a studious girl who loves to read.

Pattern

First stanza
  I am (two special characteristics you have)
  I wonder (something you are curious about)
  I hear (an imaginary sound)
  I see (an imaginary sight)
  I want (an actual desire)
  I am (the first line of the poem repeated)

Second stanza
  I pretend (something you pretend to do)
  I feel (a feeling about something imaginary)
  I touch (an imaginary touch)
  I worry (something that really bothers you)
  I cry (something that makes you very sad)
  I am (the first line of the poem repeated)

Third stanza
  I understand (something you know is true)
  I say (something you believe in)
  I dream (something you really dream about)
  I try (something you make an effort about)
  I hope (something you actually hope for)
  I am (the first line of the poem repeated)

What to do

Note: Students need to brainstorm about themselves or whatever topic they have chosen before being shown samples. With this particular poem, we have found that showing examples first tends to limit students' outlook and vocabulary as they try to imitate the sample poem rather than create a vivid description of themselves or the topic they are exploring. Examples can be used *after* they have completed their webs to see how the different items have been put together thematically.

1. Hand out a student interest web and have students generate words and phrases that describe them in terms of the web's categories.
2. Ask students to look over their webs to see whether there is a central theme that connects their special features, hopes and dreams, imaginary lives, and worries. If they find a theme, have them place it in the middle of their webs.

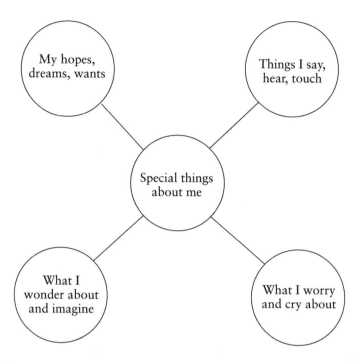

3. Show the pattern of the poem to the students. Explain that they are each going to create a poem of sentences from the words and ideas in their webs. Each line of the poem is one sentence.
4. Have the students write a first draft of their poems.
5. Have students read their drafts to see whether each line relates to the central theme they wrote in the center of the web. Suggest that they might want to make revisions so that the separate lines all relate to that theme.
6. Show examples of student-written poems and point out how other poets have expanded on the basic sentences by adding phrases and clauses in order to add details and make the poem flow smoothly.
7. Have students share their drafts and get suggestions from classmates about what details they might add.
8. More advanced learners may want to add details to their poems by adding phrases and clauses. The one- and two-word ideas from their webs have become poems.

Note: Some younger students find the starter verbs too serious or difficult to work with. See "Variations" for other options.

Uses

- to encourage self-awareness
- to demonstrate understanding of a historical figure or of a fictional character
- to personify an animal, geographical place, or other content-related concept

Variations

- For those students who find some of the starter verbs too serious or difficult to work with easily, you may want to offer options of other sensory verbs such as *smell* or *taste* instead of *touch*. Similarly, you may want to allow substitutions such as *think about* for *worry* and *laugh* or *smile* for *cry*.
- If students are writing from the point of view of a historical figure, you might want to have them change the verbs to past tense and make the poems into a kind of historical guessing game.

Student-written examples

I am a girl who loves to read.
I wonder how they could make the books.
I hear the sound of pages turning.
I see all the beautiful pictures.
I want to have a collection of books.
I am a girl who likes to read.

I pretend that I'm a book.
I feel all of the people that are in the book.
I touch a monkey in a book.
I worry that a book could break.
I cry because some books are sad.
I am a girl who likes to read.

I understand what the book is saying.
I say that this book is fun.
I dream that the book is in trouble.
I try too hard to fix the book.
I hope this book will never end.
I am a girl who loves to read.
—Ruby Carillo (age 7)

I am a sad person.
I wonder if I am liked by anyone.
I hear my parents yell at me for something I didn't do.
I see my mom telling my little brother nice things when he helps her on
    her chores.
I want to be happy at home, not sad and angry.
I am a sad person.

I pretend I don't worry about anything.
I feel sad when my mom and dad yell at me and don't yell at my
    brother.
I touch my pillow to make me happy.
I worry about my mom and dad not giving me the same love as they
    give to my little brother.
I cry when I am sad.
I am a sad person.

I understand that he is the little baby.
I only say the truth when it's true.
I dream sad things about me.
I try not to get mad at my parents.
I hope that someday I will not be treated like this.
I am a sad person
—Erendira Martinez (age 10)

I am a sphere who likes to roll.
I wonder if I can roll continuously.
I hear the sphere atoms dividing.
I see a ball rolling up a one-mile-high mountain.
I want to bounce higher than anything out there.
I am a sphere who likes to roll.

I pretend to be dunked by Michael Jordan.
I feel the pressure of air against my outer layers.
I touch the air as I am rolling.
I worry that I'll divide and never find my other half.
I cry when my friends divide.
I am a sphere who likes to roll.

I understand that not everything can roll like me.
I say all spheres should rule the earth.
I dream that I will be the first sphere president.
I try to be the best of the best.
I hope I'll never divide in two.
I am a sphere who likes to roll.
—Wendell Yazzie (age 13)

I am a girl who loves the ocean.
I wonder if I'm a mermaid.
I hear when the whale cries in the ocean.
I see the dolphins jump in the water.
I want to have a dolphin in my house.
I am a girl who loves the ocean.

I pretend to swim in the ocean with all the animals.
I feel my heart swell with the waves.
I touch a goldfish who wants to be human.
I worry about the animals' lives.
I cry when people kill whales.
I am a girl who loves the ocean.

I understand that I cannot live in the ocean.
I say my heart believes I can.
I dream my prince swims in the ocean.
I try to understand life under the sea.
I hope all people learn to love it as I do.
I am a girl who loves the ocean.
—Karen Montiel (age 13)

I am a graceful dancer.
I wonder if all the boys and girls in town like my moves.
I hear the music that makes me dance all day.
I see the people cheering for me.
I want to be one of the popular girl dancers.
I am a graceful dancer.

I pretend to be like Britney Spears.
I feel like I'm the goddess of dance.
I touch the stars and the rainbow approaching me.
I worry that my bones will get injured.
I cry if I can't move and groove.
I am a graceful dancer.

I understand that I'm not gonna be like Britney Spears or
    Christina Aguilera.
I say even though I'm not the best of all dancers, the people will like
    my style.
I dream of dancing in the clouds.
I try to please all the humans around me.
I hope that someday I will be a famous dancer.
I am a graceful dancer.
—Cristina Paredes (age 15)

I am a boy who works too hard.
I wonder if I will be a famous soccer player.
I hear the crowd cheering for me.
I see my country win the world cup.
I want to play on the El Salvador soccer team.
I am a boy who works too hard.

I pretend to be Banban Samurano.
I feel so good when I am playing soccer.
I touch the ball when defending goals.
I worry if I might break my hand.
I cry when my team loses.
I am a boy who works too hard.

I understand that not everyone is a famous soccer player.
I say next time we will win.
I dream I win a lot of medals.
I try to do my best.
I hope we win the world cup.
I am a boy who works too hard.
—Joel Bejarano (age 16)

I am an imaginative and sensitive girl.
I wonder if Prince Charming really exists.
I hear my fairy godmother speaking to me.
I see the twinkle in the stars.
I want a pumpkin coach.
I am an imaginative and sensitive girl.

I pretend to be like Cinderella.
I feel good about my dreams.
I touch my imaginary glass shoes.
I worry if Prince Charming will find me.
I cry that he won't.
I am an imaginative and sensitive girl.

I understand that Cinderella is a fairy tale.
I say that some dreams come true.
I dream that I am Cinderella.
I try to be like her.
I hope one day to meet Prince Charming.
I am an imaginative and sensitive girl.
—Iris Ohno (adult)

20 "I like" poem

Teaching points: Simple and compound sentence structure
Conjunction *but*
Negatives
Active verbs

The "I like" poem is useful for beginning English students of any age level. It models complete simple sentences, with the last sentence a compound using the conjunction *but*. It permits students to focus on likes and dislikes from their daily lives and, therefore, allows them to rehearse known vocabulary. It may be rhymed or unrhymed. Generally, the four lines describe one topic.

I like roses.	I like dogs.	We like soda.
I like pansies.	I like cats.	We like shakes.
I like marigolds,	I like horses,	We like apple juice,
but I don't like dandelions.	but I don't like rats.	but we don't like milk.

Note: The "I like" poem is similar to the contrast poem in its structure but differs in subject, verbs, and perspective. The focus of "I like" is very subjective, describing the writer's feelings and using active verbs, whereas the contrast poem is more objective, describing things apart from the writer, usually with linking verbs.

Pattern

```
I like _____.
I like _____.
I like _____,
but I don't like _____.
```

What to do

1. Before beginning the poem, make sure that students understand the idea of opposites and the use of the conjunction *but* to show opposition or contrast. Ask whether they know the opposite of *white*.

119

If they answer with *black*, try using *big* to get them to say *small*, or use *up* to get them to say *down*. To introduce or reinforce *but*, write a simple sentence such as *I like dogs*. Ask them to name another animal they like and add *and cats* (or whatever animal they name) so that the sentence reads: *I like dogs and cats*. Ask them for an animal they do not like and show them that English shows contrast or opposition with the word *but* by writing the sentence: *I like dogs, but I don't like snakes*. Point out the word *but* and the comma that separates the two clauses.

2. Explain that the students will be writing a poem about things they like and don't like. Show them the samples and point out the contrasting final line that is introduced with the word *but*. Also point out that all the lines in each poem are related by focusing on a single theme or category. Ask the students what the category for each poem is. In the poems at the beginning of this chapter, for instance, the themes are flowering plants, animals, and drinks.

3. Ask the students to name a category to help you write a sample poem or select a category that you think they will know. If the category is, for instance, ice cream, then ask the students to brainstorm all the different flavors they know. Ask them to select their three favorite flavors and help you write the first three lines of the poem:

> **Ice cream**
> We like chocolate.
> We like strawberry.
> We like vanilla

Now ask them for a flavor they don't like. Ask them what you need to do to add it as the last line of the poem. The students should be able to point out the need to add a comma after the third line and begin the fourth line with the word *but*:

> **Ice cream**
> We like chocolate.
> We like strawberry.
> We like vanilla,
> but we don't like coconut.

4. Divide the students into pairs or small groups to write their own poems. They can think of their own categories or you can pass out cards with categories already written on them. Some categories that we have used include:

music	weather	desserts	sports
games	clothing	cars	animals

5. When the students have completed their poems, have them read the poems aloud without reading the title or category. Have the other students guess what the category is.
6. Students should now be ready to write their own poems on categories of their own choice.

Uses

- to promote self-awareness
- to identify with fictional characters and historical figures

Variations

1. The "I like" contrast poem can easily be varied by changing the verb in the stem. Other stems that can be used include: *I do, I play, I read, I eat, I go,* and so on. Verbs can be varied from one sentence to the next. Also, verbs in the stems can be changed to other tenses to practice a given tense such as past tense: *I did, I ate, I went,* and so on.

I ate a squiggly crawdad.   I do the dishes
I ate a bright pink shrimp.   I empty the garbage.
I ate a spiny lobster,   I make my bed.
but I couldn't eat a snail.   I clean the table,
                                       but I don't do the ironing!

2. A second variation is as simple as adding modifying phrases to each line of the poem. For example, in the poem about chores, adverbial phrases or prepositional phrases can be added to provide detail to this simple poem:

I do the dishes every day.
I empty the garbage twice a week.
I make my bed in the morning.
I clean the table after dinner,
but I never do the ironing.

Student-written examples

Stagefright   The farm
I feel scared.   I like hens.
I feel nervous.   I like pigs.
I feel sweaty,   I like cows,
but I don't feel like I'm going to die. but I don't like all their manure.
—Noemi Torres (age 8)   —Davis Martinez (age 8)

Musical instruments
We like pianos.
We like drums.
We like violins,
but we don't like horns.
—Leslie Ramirez (age 8)

Transportation
I like cars.
I like bikes.
I like planes,
but I don't like school buses.
—Jose Almendarez (age 11)

Music
We like Latin pop.
We like reggae.
We like hip-hop,
but we don't like classic.
—Jhoselyn Alfaro (age 15),
   Marcos Martinez (age 15),
   Arturo Smith (age 15)

Animals
I like elephants.
I like cats.
I like horses,
but I don't like rats.
 – Nancy Lopez (adult)

Food
I like Mexican food like *pozole* and *sopes*.
I like Taco Bell burritos, tostados, and tacos.
I like Chinese egg rolls and fried rice,
but I don't like white beans.
—Rosa Pacheco (adult)

Boats
I like motorboats.
I like sailboats.
I like the Titanic,
but I don't like icebergs.
—Anthony Gonzalez (age 8)

Activities
I like to play soccer.
I like to swim in the pool.
I like to ride my bike,
but I don't like to run.
—Daniel Felix (age 12)

Sports
We like to play soccer.
We like to play basketball.
We like to play tennis,
but we don't like to play
   volleyball.
—Arturo Caro (age 16), Luz
   Yadira Melendez (age 16),
   Juan Carlos Reyes (age 15)

School
I like English.
I like science class.
I like dance class,
but I don't like mathematics.
—Cady Rueda (adult)

21 "I wish" poem

Teaching points: Structures following *wish*
Tense in conditional clauses
Noun clauses

Wish poems generally have a theme such as appearance, food, friendship, place, or activities; however, a theme is not required for the poem to have a pleasing and effective result. They are usually four or five lines long (although they can be much longer), with each unrhymed line beginning with "I wish." Students have the option of adding a final line to summarize their wishes.

I wish I were a big black stallion.
I wish I had a mane of golden
    vines.
I wish I could gallop across the
    prairie.
I wish I would never come home.
Then freedom would be my name.

I wish I weren't so rubbery.
I wish I weren't so pink.
I wish kids wouldn't chew on me
When they try to think.

I wish for taco-flavored ice cream.
I wish for chocolate-covered bees'
    knees.
I wish I had a mint pancake.
I wish I had honey-covered fried
    chicken.
I wish I had an ice-cream pizza.

Pattern

Line 1: I wish . . .
Line 2: I wish . . .
Line 3: I wish . . .
Line 4: I wish . . .
Line 5: Conclusion (optional)

Lesson 21

What to do

1. Ask students to think about what they would wish for if they had one wish at this moment. Ask them to write their wish on a piece of paper. Ask for volunteers who are willing to share their wishes with the rest of the class. As students say their wishes, write a complete sentence for each wish on the board, modeling the correct structures. Try to vary the verbs you use as much as possible (I wish I could . . . , I wish I had . . . , I wish I were . . . , I wish to go . . . , I wish for . . . , etc.).

2. Have students examine the sentences you have written. Ask them to notice the verbs in each sentence. Underline verb phrases as they identify them. Depending on the level of your students, at this point you may want to discuss or reinforce the usage of verbs in conditional clauses. If students are not ready for direct grammatical instruction, at least you will have various patterns on the board that they can use.

3. Using one of the examples the students gave, explain that poems usually give vivid imagery through detail. Ask students to use their sense of smell, touch, taste, sight, and hearing to come up with details for their wishes. For instance, if a student wished for a hot dog, you might ask how he or she likes the hot dog: with ketchup, mustard, chili, onions, or other condiments. The wish might change from "I wish I had a hot dog" to "I wish I had a hot dog, dripping with chili and onions." If a student wished for a pony, ask what the pony looks and feels like. The sentence might evolve from "I wish I had a pony" to "I wish I had a pony with a silky brown coat and a mane that flows with the wind."

4. Now tell students that you are going to write a wish poem together. Ask them to select one of the wishes on the board and name a general topic for it, or ask them for suggestions of topics that would interest many people. If it is before break or lunch, you might ask them to think about foods that they like as that topic might stimulate enthusiastic responses! Write the topic on the board.

5. Tell students that there are no limits to their wishes. Ask them to use their imaginations to conjure up something related to the topic.

6. Pair up students and give each pair a few minutes to think of a detailed wish. Write the words and phrases students create on the board, arranging them randomly rather than linearly.

7. After the students have generated a long list of items, show them some examples of the "I wish" poem. Draw their attention to the use of different verbs to express wishes and to the order of the wishes in the poem. Explain that some wish poems can have a concluding sentence that does not necessarily begin with "I wish."

8. Ask the pairs of students to join another pair to create groups of four. Ask the students to select the wishes they like from among those

124

previously generated and to arrange them in a pleasing order on the handout, with one wish after each "I wish" stem. Tell them that they can add more detail and a concluding sentence if they like.

Note: At this point, it might be helpful to distribute handouts with the beginning of the sentence stem "I wish . . ." prewritten in 4 or 5 lines.

9. Have each group read its "I wish" poem to the class. Students are now ready to write their own poems.

Uses

- to introduce personal goal setting
- to identify with the feelings of another person, character, or animal
- to personify an inanimate object
- to promote self-awareness

Variations

1. Instead of using *I wish* to begin each line of the poem, students may use *I think, I hope, I dream, I believe* (or other similar verbs). A single verb may be repeated in the same poem, or verbs can be mixed to reflect the thoughts of the writer. For example:

I think I must be crazy.   I dream I am an angel.
I think I must be nuts.   I think I am a perfect one.
I think I'm being silly.   I believe I'll fly through the moon-lit
I think I'm just in love.   night.
                                            I hope this dream will always be.

2. Lines of the poem can be adapted in any way to show the writer's feelings. For example, conjunctions or subordinators can be used to show cause/effect or consequence. The last line of the poem can be used to show juxtaposition or to bring the "wishful" thinking back into the real world:

I wish I had more money
So that I could buy you beautiful things.
I wish I had more time
So that I could be with you more often.
I wish for many wishes
That will never come true.
But my wishes – and my love – for you will never end.

3. Words and phrases can be added before the stem to vary the pattern:

In the morning, I wish I could stay in bed till noon.
At noon, I dream of cookies and milk after school.
After school, I hope some friends stop by my house to play.
At the house, I think about my homework while I watch TV till bedtime.
At bedtime, I wish I could stay up all night.

Student-written examples

A fairy-tale life
I wish I were a beautiful princess.
I wish I had gold and treasure.
I wish I could go to the ball.
I wish I had a huge, towered castle.
Life would be fantastic!
—Elizabeth Gordon Taylor's class (ages 6 and 7)

Unreal wishes
I wish my baby sister would grow faster.
I wish school didn't have to stop for vacation.
I wish I had a lot of pets.
I wish my handwriting were good.
I wish for lots of things that will never change.
—Gemma Andaya (age 8)

Wishing for words
I wish to be a good person when I grow up.
I wish to become a citizen of the U.S.A. some day.
I wish I could speak any language.
I wish I had a good friend to talk to.
Then I would be happy for my whole life.
—Ler Say Htay (age 13)

School
I wish there were no school.
I wish there were no rules.
I wish we could chew gum.
I wish we had no homework.
I wish all teachers were nice.
I wish I could just talk and play with my friends all day long.
—Erica Ramos (age 11)

Speed
I wish I had a bicycle.
I wish I had a motorcycle.
I wish I had a car.
I wish I could go fast.
Then I would have fun.
—Yeri Soleria (age 13)

Culinary delights
We wish we had a roasted pig with an apple in its mouth,
  Crispy skin, juicy meat, and a sweet sauce.
We wish we had enchiladas made with delicious corn tortillas,
  Tender juicy chicken, spicy red sauce, lettuce, and sour cream.
We wish we had a big tray of *asado* – beef, chicken, pork,
  Peppers, onions, and hot tomato sauce
  Roasted over hot coals and smelling like smoke.
We wish we had a steak dripping with juice,
  Complete with onions and an Italian salad.
We wish we had a *pupusa* with dripping white cheese,
  Red plum beans, shredded beef, and *curtido*.
And finally, we wish we had a giant banana split dripping with
  Whipped cream, nuts, and three kinds of syrup.
—Joannie Monroy's class (ages 14 to 17)

Homecoming
I wish I could fly like a bird.
I would go as far as the moon.
I wish I could swim like a fish.
I would glide around the world.
I wish I could go far away,
And then I would wish to come
  home.
—Sneha Patel (age 15),
  Lucy Lopez (age 16),
  Leonardo Cejas (age 14),
  Javier Camarena (age 15)

Food
I wish I had some mole.
I wish I had guacamole.
I wish I had a pozole.
But instead I got cannoli.
—Monica Espinoza (adult)

You
How I wish you had been so
  generous.
How I wish you had been so
  genial.
How I wish you had been so gentle.
But I loved you nonetheless.
—Hiroshi Iris (adult)

Love
I think love is waiting for phone
  calls.
I think love is sharing problems.
I think love is paying the bills.
I think love is as simple as
  washing the dishes.
—Hyunkoo Kim (adult)

Boyfriend
I wish I had a boyfriend.
I hope I'll have one soon.
I hope that he's an alien
Coming from the moon.
—Monica Espinoza (adult)

To be with you
I wish I had wings.
I wish I had an Aladdin's carpet.
I wish I had a witch's broom
So that I could fly to you every
  night.
If only wishes came true.
—Hiroshi Iris (adult)

22 Phrase poem

Teaching points: Verb phrases
Verb, noun, and prepositional phrases
Clauses
Parallel structure

The phrase poem can be used to reinforce almost any type of phrase or clause while creating an image of a particular topic or scene. Because most of the lines in these list-like poems are the same structure, they can also be used to teach parallel structure in a series of items.

Floating in the air,
Gliding through the garden,
Drinking from the flowers,
Dancing on the leaves,
Landing on my finger,
Butterflies are free.

Hot chocolate steaming,
Rich aroma rising,
White marshmallows melting,
Cold hands grasping,
Big cup waiting,
Cocoa in winter tastes good.

Pattern

Line 1: Specific phrase or clause
Line 2: Same type of phrase or clause
Line 3: Same type of phrase or clause
Line 4: Same type of phrase or clause
Line 5: Same type of phrase or clause
Line 6: Subject of phrases or clauses

What to do

1. Decide on the structure students need to practice. The first sample poem above, for instance, establishes a pattern of present participle + prepositional phrase; the pattern of the second sample is adjective + noun + present participle.
2. Divide students into small groups and give each group a picture. The picture may be of a subject they have studied, a character in a story,

128

a season or holiday, a geometric concept, or anything else that is relevant.

3. Ask students to write down facts and impressions about their group's picture.
4. Show the students the structure you want them to practice and, perhaps, a sample poem using that structure.
5. Have students revise the facts and impressions to fit the structure.
6. Have students arrange their phrases in a logical sequence and then write the subject of the phrases on the last line, as either a noun phrase or a subject-verb clause.
7. When students have finished, have them share their poems by reading them aloud, perhaps omitting the last line so that other students can guess their subject.
8. Students should now be ready to write their own phrase poems individually.

Uses

- to summarize knowledge about a specific subject area (e.g., seasons, math concepts, animals)
- to describe a fictional character
- to summarize a story

Variations

1. Begin with the topic on the first line and add to it with prepositional phrases and a concluding line that makes a statement about the topic:

Faces
Of a baby with chubby cheeks,
Of a child with tears rolling down her face,
Of a red-nosed clown,
Of the glowing moon at night,
Of my own fears,
Are the faces I most remember.

2. Begin with the topic and *is* or *are* to define a topic with noun and participial phrases:

Winter is
Spotless snow shimmering in the sun,
Ice-skaters gliding across the frozen pond,
Puffs in the air following every breath,
Icicles hanging from every branch of trees,
Hot cocoa warming the chill you have inside.

3. Begin with the last line as a summary such as "These are the things that drive me crazy" or "These are my favorite things" or "This was the life of . . ." and then create the phrase structure and list of items that fit the summary:

People who get in my way,
Bugs that fly around my head,
Phrases that make my tongue get twisted,
People who crack their gum,
Brothers who always have to be right,
These are the things that drive me crazy.

Note: Almost any type of phrase or clause can be used in this poem without changing the pattern:

- participle + adverb (*Running quickly*)
- participle + prepositional phrase (*Running down the street*)
- verb infinitive (*To run*)
- imperative statements (*Run for your life!*)
- conditional clause (*If we run fast*)

The final line, however, should fit the type of phrase or clause selected.

Student-written examples

Walking across the piano,
Playing with yarn,
Eating tuna salad,
Running on the carpet,
Sitting on the furniture,
Sleeping on a bed,
Scratching at the curtains,
Cats are mischievous animals.
—Roxana Cano (age 9), Neydi Contreras (age 9)

Swinging from branch to branch,
Living in the green forest,
Eating bananas all day,
Chattering with a loud voice,
Screeching while doing turns in the air,
Dreaming to be a gorilla,
Monkeys like to be free.
—Jennifer Villatoro (age 9)

Colorful flowers blooming,
Seeds spreading through the sky,
Bears coming out of hibernation,
Rabbits eating delicious plants,
Children playing outdoor games,
Families enjoying their vacation,
Light showers watering new plants,
Springtime has arrived.
—Xochitl Nava (age 9)

Fighting battles in Star Wars,
Screaming through the stars in Space Mountain,
Running from fires and dangerous snakes with Indiana Jones,
Being scared in the Haunted House by ghosts and dead people from
      a cemetery,
Visiting Mickey Mouse's house and shaking his hand in Toon Town,
Working with seven midgets on Snow White's ride,
Battling and fighting the ships in the Pirates of the Caribbean,
Flying around in little rockets up and down in Tomorrowland,
Racing future cars through dark tunnels with colorful lights,
Circling the jungle all around the theme park on the train . . .
We'll have fun at Disneyland!
—Lance Egan's class (ages 11 to 13)

Soccer players kicking and butting the ball
Swimmers crawling, stroking, butterflying,
Horses running and jumping,
Gymnasts twisting, somersaulting, and rolling,
Boxers punching, blocking, and ducking . . .
The summer Olympics are the best sports and a union for all countries.
—Claudette Willems's class (ages 14 to 17)

Dancing in the pure world,
Wearing garments like queens and kings,
Dreaming of flying in the blue sky,
Giving to people a lot of comfort,
Sleeping with their big, round eyes open,
Gulping with their mouths like a wordy chatterbox,
The great tropical fish enjoy their lives!
—Emi Sugiyama, Hyesook Moon (adults)

Traveling around the world with my camera,
Sunbathing at the beach with a piña colada in my hand,
Sleeping until noon with no regret,
Swimming in the ocean and becoming a fish,
Forgetting the time and feeling like a child,
Reading a good novel that takes me away to another place,
Eating delicious seafood while listening to the sounds of the sea,
Vacations are made of this!
–Susana Gonzalez, Kat Zdeb Toczynska, Marlene Onate (adults)

Flowing from everyone's mouth,
Expressing the deepest and the most superficial feelings,
Making get-togethers joyful,
Being lovely and stern,
Communicating with people back and forth around the world,
Taking for granted when you know and making you cry when you
    don't,
That's what language puts you through.
—Marta Oliveira, Jessica Mungia (adults)

23 Preposition poem

Teaching points: Prepositions and prepositional phrases
Sequencing

The preposition poem is a fun way to introduce prepositions and prepositional phrases. It includes as many prepositional phrases as needed, in just one or two sentences, to describe an object or narrate an event. Although it has no set length, we recommend that students use at least five prepositional phrases in their poems.

Over the wall,	Between the crowded ticket lines,
Under the plant,	Behind the smelly hot-dog stand,
Onto the stones,	Around the circling Ferris wheel,
The grasshopper jumped.	Beyond the fortune teller's tent, and
	Through the house of mirrors,
	I searched for my kid brother.

Pattern

> Line 1: Prepositional phrase
> Line 2: Prepositional phrase
> Line 3: Prepositional phrase
> Line 4: Prepositional phrase
> Line 5: Prepositional phrase
> Line 6: Main clause about an event or object

What to do

1. First, have students generate a list of prepositions that they know. An easy way to do this is to use examples that can illustrate different functions of prepositions (place and direction, for instance). To illustrate place prepositions, for example, use a small object such as a pencil. Ask students where the object is being placed each time you move it (on the desk, under the desk, beside the desk, in the desk, etc.). For directional prepositions, ask students, "Where does a bird fly?" (Up into the sky, over the clouds, through the air, past a tree, etc.).

2. As the students generate the prepositions, write them on the board where students will be able to refer to them later. Below is a list of words commonly used as prepositions that can be used for guidance:

about	behind	from	toward
above	below	in	under
across	beneath	into	underneath
after	beside	of	until
against	between	off	up
along	beyond	on	upon
among	by	over	with
around	down	through	within
at	except	throughout	without
before	for	to	

(For more advanced learners, you might also want to introduce groups of words that act as prepositions: *in spite of, on account of, due to,* etc.).

3. Show the students several samples of preposition poems and ask them what they notice about the first word of each line. They should be able to recognize prepositions they have just named and/or add to the list of prepositions on the board.

4. Ask students to identify what the poem does (tells a story) and how many sentences it has (usually just one). Also ask them to identify the sequence (a series of prepositional phrases until the last line or two, which tell the story).

5. Explain that prepositions are used all the time to explain such things as where events take place or when something happens. Have an example in mind to demonstrate how to create a preposition poem. For instance, with the students helping you think up phrases, you might describe how students get to your classroom:

> Down the hall,
> around the corner,
> past the drinking fountain,
> through the door marked 132,
> into the classroom
> the students come.

6. Before students write their own poems, show them more examples and help them think of ideas so that not all the poems are about getting to a particular place. They should then be ready to begin writing their own poems as individuals, in pairs, or in small groups.

Uses

- to demonstrate understanding of an animal, math concept, or other content-related term
- to narrate events in a story
- to describe a character
- to describe a scientific or other process

Variations

1. For more advanced students, you might want to arrange your phrasing differently, allowing the prepositions to fall in the middle of the line rather than at the beginning. For instance, an extension of the classroom poem given earlier ("Down the hall . . .") might look like this:

There they sit,
looking *at* books,
writing *on* paper,
daydreaming *in* their heads,
glancing *out* the window,
playing *with* toys
until it's time *to* go home.

2. Use the same preposition repeatedly to show sequencing logic. For instance, the following poem shows a progression from specific to general (though it could also be reversed):

Here I sit
In my pajamas,
In a chair,
In my room,
In my house,
In the suburbs,
Trying to write a poem.

Student-written examples

Across the blanket
Over the grass
Under the tree
Green bugs look for something
    to eat.
—Danny Diaz (age 6)

Into an old hut,
Over the cold, slow water,
Around the tree trunks,
Through the green forest,
Between the branches and vines,
Across the purple orchids,
Under the grasses and soil,
Behind the leaves and rocks,
The boa constrictor slithers.
—Elizabeth Gordon Taylor's
    class (ages 6 and 7)

Through the dark wet mist,
Beside the rushing river,
Into gigantic, beautiful trees,
Close to toucans and big, wet
    leaves,
We got lost in the rain forest.
—Pairisblu Davis (age 9),
    Neydi Contreras (age 9)

From the stations,
Through the radio,
On the air,
Into our cars,
Down our legs,
The music makes us dance.
—Jose Barajas (age 12),
    Irvin Hervis (age 11),
    Xuan Vo (age 12),
    Sasha Babic (age 13)

Into the hot oil,
Around the cooker, flying
Up into the air,
Inside the bag,
Down the aisle,
By my seat,
I take a bag of popcorn to
    my girl.
—Benyam Hailemariam (age 13),
    Alan Thirion (age 13)

Under the water
Beside the long, green seaweed,
Above the slimy sea worms,
Below the alarming boat,
Around the big rock,
The butterfly dolphin gracefully
    splashes.
—Amy Moreno (age 9),
    Abella Rutahindurwa (age 9)

Through the berry bushes
Past the tall trees,
Between the small hills
Beside the vast lake,
Across the roaring jungle,
The jaguar reaches its
    destination.
—Gabrielle McAdory (age 9)

Out of the hole,
Up the ramp,
Around the corner,
Against the flippers,
Beside the bumpers,
Behind the pictures,
Into the lights,
Across from the toy people,
The pinball goes into the hole
    and I score!
—Philmon Girmay (age 11),
    Gerardo Novoa (age 13),
    Milan Kodic (age 13)

After we ate
On the beach
Under an umbrella
About five
In the afternoon,
Mariela went swimming
And was eaten
By a shark.
—Jorge Ordaz (age 15),
    Mariela Bailon (age 16),
    Chris Fugrad (age 16)

In the living room
Across the hall
Under the stairs
Beside the kitchen
On top of the table
Behind the door,
Everyone was dancing and
    having fun.
—Maria Ordoñez (age 17),
  Neha Chada (age 16),
  Beatriz Saenz (age 18)

The wedding
As the music starts, all eyes look
down the red carpet
to the beautiful bride walking
forward to the altar
with a happy face;
within a few minutes, the scared
    groom waits
on the blessing that will tie him
for the rest of his life!
—Susana Gonzalez, Mosammat
  Khanom (adults)

Mr. Frog's last day
With a big mouth singing like Ricky Martin
on a lily pad
under the hot sun, jumping
into the water, swimming around happily, diving
down deep
in the water, Mr. Frog collided
with a crocodile who ate him all
up!
—Mikyoung Lee, Unyoung Son,
  Jung Hee Lee (adults)

24 Simile poem

Teaching points: Similes
Sentence structure
Analytical thinking (breaking items into parts)
Possessive pronouns

The simile poem can be short or long depending on the person or object that is its focus. It can also be written from a first-, second-, or third-person point of view, again depending on the focus and the writer's perspective. Funny or serious, each line is usually a complete sentence. Sometimes, however, the poem may read better when the sentence is continued on another line (as in the second model below).

Your face is like an angel's, beautiful to look at.
Your hips are like a pendulum, swaying with the music.
Your music is like the sunshine, brightening my day.
You, Ricky Martin, are my idol.

My hair is like a terra cotta pot, reddish brown and blazing in the sun.
My eyes are like glimmering brown sequins, merrily viewing the world.
My cheeks are like pink cotton candy, soft but with a few crinkles
     from age.
My mouth is like a flower, opening up to greet my friends
Through the white picket fence of my teeth
And the red carnations of my lips.

Pattern

Line 1: (Possessive pronoun) (feature) is like . . .
Line 2: (Possessive pronoun) (feature) is like . . .
Line 3: (Possessive pronoun) (feature) is like . . .
Line 4: (Possessive pronoun) (feature) is like . . .
Line 5: Optional summary ending

Note: Depending on the topic and point of view selected, any of the possessive pronouns may be used: *my, our, your, his, her, its, their.*

What to do

1. Explain that in colloquial English we often ask "What's it like" and rarely get an answer to our question. For instance, someone might say, "I bought a new coat." The other person would say, "What's it like?" Instead of comparing it, as the word *like* implies, the first speaker describes it: "It's blue with gold buttons." Similarly, a person might say, "I just met a new boy at school." The other person would probably say, "What's he like?" Again, instead of comparing the boy to others, the first speaker says, "Oh, he's really nice."

2. Now explain that the students are going to write a poem that really does answer the question "What's it like?"

3. Ask the students to name the features of the face (hair, eyes, nose, lips, teeth, cheeks, eyebrows, ears, etc.). Write the words in a column on the board.

4. Show a picture of a person, preferably someone with whom the students are familiar, and ask the students to select four or five of the person's features that they think are the best or most interesting.

   Note: If you think your students would be comfortable writing about themselves, you can skip the picture and ask students to select four or five features of their own. To model writing the poem, you would need to select four or five features of your own. Another alternative is to use a picture of an animal, a fruit, a flower, and so on, and to identify the features of the object (they may vary from human features) before selecting the ones to write about. The poem can be written from any point of view in the first person, second person, or third person. Some of the samples and student-written examples illustrate these variations.

5. Have the students write the words they selected in a column, with each word preceded by the word *His* or *Her* (depending on your picture), as you do the same on the board:

   > His hair
   > His eyes
   > His chin
   > His ears

6. Next have the students add "is like" or "are like" after each item as you write it on the board:

   > His hair is like
   > His eyes are like
   > His chin is like
   > His ears are like

7. Now show the students examples of the poem and have them identify the pattern that they will be following.
8. Have the students help you create the poem by telling what the features in the picture are like. If students offer only a word or two, ask for details to explain. For instance, when students said the teacher's hair was "like a terra cotta pot" (in the sample at the beginning of this lesson), she asked for more detail, and the students added that it was "reddish brown" and that it "kind of blazes in the sun." When the comparisons are complete, ask the students to add a summary for the last line, telling who the person is (as in the Ricky Martin example at the beginning of this lesson: "You, Ricky Martin, are my idol.").
9. Divide the students into small groups to write their own poems.

    Note: If you are prepared with pictures of people, animals, or objects (one for each group), students will have a focus to help them get started more quickly.

10. When the poems are complete, have the students share them by reading them aloud to the class.

Uses

• to encourage self-awareness by describing oneself
• to describe a food, animal, nonhuman object, or abstract concept
• to describe a famous person or historical figure
• to describe any aspect of nature (a mountain, a river, etc.)

Variations

1. If you want to emphasize the difference between similes and metaphors, have students rewrite their poems, leaving out the word *like:*

    My hair is an angel's halo, circling around my face.
    My eyes are an eagle, seeing far and wide.
    My chin is a mule; it stubbornly sticks out when I demand my way.
    My ears are radar, hearing everything around me.
    I am a teacher, kind but demanding, who sees and hears my students
        even when they think I don't.

2. If you want to emphasize analytical thinking, use inanimate objects and ask students to identify features (since the objects probably will not actually have eyes, ears, mouth, etc.). If the object is named only in the last line, students often like to play a kind of guessing game

by not reading aloud the final line, which is a good test of their analytical and descriptive abilities:

My body is like a mirror that shimmers in the sun.
My touch is soft as silk, soothing all alike.
My shape twists and turns like a snake moving along a path.
My mouth opens wide like a door left ajar
And greets the ocean with glad tidings every day.
I am a river, meandering, wet, and refreshing.

Student-written examples

Its skin is soft and fuzzy like a bunny's fur.
It tastes sweet like sugar.
Its color is like the sun in the morning.
Its shape is round like a ball.
It is a peach, my favorite fruit.
—Manuel Botello (age 7)

My hair is as soft as a cotton ball.
My eyes are as round as marbles.
My cheeks are like soft gum.
My mouth is like a cave inside.
My face is flat like a table.
—Antonio Arias (age 8)

My eyes are shiny like a black car in the middle of the desert.
My lips are red like the color of the flag of my country.
My eyebrows are like a seagull flying in my face.
My mouth is like a black hole in the universe.
I'm a kid who wants to run like a jaguar.
—Alan Thirion (age 13)

My hair is spiky like a porcupine.
My eyes are round like a ball.
My cheeks are pink like a strawberry.
My mouth is like a hole.
My face is brown like a football.
– Luis Rubio (age 8)

My hair is like a desert, brown.
My tongue is like a heart, red.
My cheeks are like a cute princess.
My lips are like a beautiful rose.
I'm a happy person who walks in the rainbow when the rain ends.
—Karen Montiel (age 13)

His hair is like a shiny yellow sun.
His eyes are blue like the sky.
His lips are hot like a fire.
His teeth are white like the snow.
He is Justin, a hot 'N Sync singer who makes me crazy.
—Eliza Hunanyan (age 12)

My eyes are gold and dark like the moon.
My fur is smooth and soft like the petals of a rose.
My whiskers are white like fear.
My ears are pointy like a pyramid.
I am a mysterious cat.
—Mariano Alba (age 15), Jim Gacula (age 18),
    Oscar Miranda (age 16), Oscar Morales (age 17)

My eyes are small like tears.
My nose is big like a black heart.
My fur is golden like the sun.
My eyebrows are curved like a question mark.
My ears are soft like a powder puff.
I'm a golden retriever puppy.
—Daisy Camarena (age 15), Rocio Mora (age 16),
    Marisol Cisneros (age 17)

It's bright like a star in the dark night.
It has many faces like the moon.
It's clear like water.
Its value is like a loving woman's heart.
It's the symbol of love for all women that is unchanged forever.
It's a diamond.
—Emi Sugiyama, Mikyoung Lee, Unyoung Son (adults)

My eyes are like marbles.
My nose is like a black egg.
My ears are like powder puffs.
My fur is soft like a carpet of grass.
I am a koala bear, the symbol of Australia
—Vanhdala Keomalavong (age 17), Sandra Gonzalez (age 14),
    Linhnaphone Bouaravong (age 17)

We are like a couple in love; we go everywhere together.
We are like twins; we help and follow each other step-by-step.
We are like a family; we have ten kids who are our most
     precious treasure.
We are like the ocean that sometimes runs away from home,
     then runs back.
Who are we?
We are your feet!
—Marta Oliveira, Susana Gonzalez (adults)

My face is red like blood and soft like velvet.
My body is thin like a straw.
My arms flow in the wind like birds.
My smell is sweet like a first kiss.
My thorns are sharp like needles.
My leaves are green like the rain forest.
I am the red, red rose.
—Kat Zdeb Toczynska, Mosammat F. Khanom (adults)

My skin is wrinkled and yellow like a weak, old lady.
My shape is round like a withered ball.
My flesh is jellied like the human being's heart.
My taste is sour and sweet like a broken romance.
My name is passion fruit.
—Marta Oliveira, Susana Gonzalez (adults)

25 Who-what-where-when-why-how poem

Teaching points: Complete sentences
Sequencing information
Phrases (verb, noun, adjective, adverb,
    prepositional)
Summarizing

The who-what-where-when-why-how poem is a pleasingly arranged summary of information broken into phrases that form a single sentence. It transforms the six basic questions of good journalism into a poetic format.

Maria's family
went to Paris
in France
on a plane
during summer vacation
so they could see the Eiffel Tower.

The United States of America
declared its independence in 1776
and became a country of its own
by fighting off the British
because its people wanted freedom.

Romeo and Juliet
killed themselves
in fair Verona
many years ago,
he by poison, she by knife,
because their families would not tolerate each other.

Cinderella
found her Prince Charming
at the ball
before the stroke of midnight
because her fairy godmother helped her
look so beautiful.

Pattern

> Answer the questions for each line:
> Line 1: Who? Name a person or object.
> Line 2: What? Begin with a verb to describe an event.
> Line 3: Where? Tell where the event occurred.
> Line 4: When? Tell when the event occurred.
> Line 5: How? Tell how the event occurred.
> Line 6: Why? Explain why the event occurred.
>
> *Note:* The order of the questions/lines can be
> rearranged to make the sentence flow better.

What to do

1. Ask students to name the six main words with which questions begin. If they have studied newspapers, you might want to remind them that these are the same questions that are used in good journalism (*who, what, where, when, why,* and *how*). Write the six words in a row (not a column) on the board.
2. Explain that students will be writing a poem answering these questions about a person or character. Show them some sample poems and have them identify which question each line answers. Point out that the same order is not always used. Ask them how many sentences the entire poem takes (one).
3. If students do not have a common background to be able to work with a fictional character or historical person, select a short story to read to them. We have used very brief versions of different Aesop fables such as "The Hare and the Tortoise" and "The Fox and the Crow." If students also have a copy of the story, tell them to follow along carefully in order to be able to answer the six questions.
4. When you have finished reading the story aloud, point to the six questions written on the board and ask the students to answer them. Under *who*, write the name(s) they state. Ask the students to respond to the other questions about the same story by asking, "What did he or she do that is important to know?" Add to the other question words the same way ("When did he or she do it?" "Where?" "How did he or she do it?" "Why did he or she do it?").
5. Tell the students that now that all the facts are known, you want to arrange them into a poetic form that also makes a complete sentence. Ask for suggestions as to which line should come first and then which should come next until all the parts are in an order that should work into a sentence.

6. If the lines do not work out into a logical and complete sentence, ask the students to help revise the lines until they do become a sentence. They may need to revise the wording or change the order of the lines. For instance, the first draft of a who-what-where-when-why-how poem may begin by looking like this:

> The hare and the tortoise
> ran a race
> one afternoon
> on a winding path
> to pass the time.
> The slow tortoise beat the fast hare
> > because the hare stopped to rest.

But it may end up like this:

> One summer afternoon
> a tortoise
> won a race against a hare
> along a winding path
> because the tortoise kept going
> while the hare stopped to rest.

7. Have students write their own poems in small groups and then share them with the rest of the class by reading them aloud.
8. Students should now be ready to practice writing their own poems.

Uses

- to introduce each student and an important event in the student's life as an icebreaker
- to define or describe a historic event, an animal, a geographic location, or other content-related concept or idea
- to summarize the plot of a story
- to describe a character, well-known person, or historical figure

Student-written examples

The very hungry caterpillar
Ate a lot of junk food
Outside in the grass at the park
During one week
Because he was very hungry.
—Elizabeth Gordon Taylor's
   class (ages 6 and 7)

Hagrid helped
Harry Potter
To go to wizard school
At Hogwarts
In 1989
To learn magic.
—Abraham Rodriguez (age 9),
   Randy Aleman (age 8)

One afternoon
Three little pigs
Went to build their houses
With straw, sticks, and bricks
In the wood
So they could be safe.
—Davis Martinez (age 8)

At Kent State University
On April 30, 1970
Students
Protested and four were killed
By the National Guard
Because President Nixon sent
    more soldiers to Vietnam.
—Ernesto Pineda (age 13),
  Anh Pham (age 11),
  Rosario Garcia (age 13)

Mike Tyson
Bit Holyfield's ear
During a fight
In 1997
Because he was angry
But he got the money anyway.
—Ler Say Htay (age 12),
  Cesar Sosa (age 11),
  Ler Law Lah Htay (age 13)

Carlos Santana
won eight awards
at the Grammy ceremony
in February 2000
because he is the best guitar player
who follows his heart.
—Oscar Miranda (age 16),
  Oscar Morales (age 17),
  Mariano Alba (age 15),
  Jim Gacula (age 18)

Michael Jordan
The best NBA player
Retired
From the Chicago Bulls
In 1998
To enjoy his money.
—Alvaro Villalobos (age 12),
  Alex Villalobos (age 11),
  Radomir Rakic (age 11)

Benito Juarez
Fought the French
With farm tools
In Mexico
In 1862
Because he wanted the French
    to leave Mexico.
—Laura Gamboa (age 11),
  Elvisdiela Guzman (age 12)

A long time ago
in ancient China
Mulan
pretended to be a soldier
by dressing in a boy's clothing
so that her father would not
    have to fight.
—Vanhdala Keomalavong
  (age 17), Linhnaphone
  Bouaravong (age 17),
  Sandra Gonzalez (age 14)

Santa Claus
came to Las Vegas
to give presents
on December 25th
but refused to stay
because it was so hot!
—Kyung Joon Kim (adult)

Banana, the king of fruit,
was eaten by me
after I cut his body and covered him with honey
in my kitchen
this morning
because he wanted to go to my stomach.
—Emi Sugiyama (adult)

Sinyoung and Jaehoo
met each other
in the class of their university
four years ago and
got married
because they loved each other.
—Unyoung Son (adult)

Many years ago,
Antoine de Saint-Exupéry
wrote my favorite story, *The Little Prince,*
about the universe
because love and friendship are forever
when people want it.
—Marlene Onate (adult)

Glossary

Abstract noun. *See* Noun, abstract.

Adjective. A word used to describe a noun (e.g., *big* dog, *green* car, *good* idea, *ten* dollars).

Adverb. A word used to describe a verb, adjective, or other adverb (e.g., he walked *slowly,* a *bright* red shirt, he walked *very* slowly).

Alliteration. Repetition of beginning and dominant consonant sounds in words of close proximity (e.g., the hard *c* or *k* sound in "the clumsy kangaroo quickly cantered toward the cool water").

Analogy. A comparison (e.g., *her eyes sparkled like diamonds*).

Analytical thinking. Thinking that breaks a concept or object into its component parts.

Antithesis. Rhetorical contrast of two ideas.

Antonym. A word of opposite meaning (e.g., *good/bad*).

Auxiliary verb. *See* Verb, auxiliary.

Brainstorming. A writing technique that involves the spontaneous contribution of ideas from all members of the group.

Cardinal number. *See* Number, cardinal.

Clause. A group of words containing a subject and predicate and used as part or all of a sentence.

Clause, conditional. A subordinate or dependent clause expressing under what conditions the main clause occurs (e.g., "*If you pass the test,* you will pass the course"). Subordinate conjunctions that express condition include *although, provided, unless, if.*

Clause, coordinate. A main (independent) clause attached to another main (independent) clause by use of a coordinate conjunction (*and, but, yet, nor, or, for, so*) (e.g., "Betty had broken her arm, but *she competed in the race anyway*").

Clause, dependent. *See* Clause, subordinate.

Clause, independent. *See* Clause, main.

Clause, main. Expresses a complete thought and can stand alone as a sentence (e.g., "Betty couldn't compete in the race"). Also called an independent clause.

Clause, noun. A subordinate or dependent clause used as a single noun (e.g., "I can't remember *what he said*").

Clause, subordinate. Does not express a complete thought because it is attached to a main clause by use of a subordinate conjunction (*after, because, since, while,* etc.) (e.g., "Betty couldn't compete in the race *because she had broken her arm*"). Also called a dependent clause.

Comma in compound sentence. *See* Compound sentence.

Compound sentence. A sentence composed of two complete sentences joined by a coordinate conjunction (*and, but, yet, nor, or, for, so*) (e.g., *Bob went to* *see a movie, but it was sold out.*) A compound sentence requires a comma before the conjunction that joins the two sentences.

Concrete noun. *See* Noun, concrete.

Conditional clause. *See* Clause, conditional.

Conjunction. A word that joins together sentences, clauses, phrases, or words. Coordinate conjunctions include *and, but, yet, nor, or, for, so.* Subordinate conjunctions include *after, although, as, as if, as long as, as though, because, before, if, in order that, since, so that, than, though, unless, until, when, whenever, where, wherever, while.*

Coordinate clause. *See* Clause, coordinate.

Dependent clause. *See* Clause, subordinate.

Determiner. A word that specifies a noun (e.g., *a, an, the, this, that*), quantifies a noun (e.g., *five, ten, some, all, several*), or makes a noun possessive (e.g., *my, his, her, their*).

First-person pronoun/verb. The verb in a sentence must agree with the person of the subject of the sentence; that is, a first-person singular subject (*I*) must use a first-person singular verb (*am, have, like,* etc.). A first-person plural subject (*we*) must use a first-person plural verb (*are, have, like,* etc.).

Five senses. Common reference to the senses of sight, smell, hearing, taste, and touch.

Idiom. Language particular to a people or area. An idiomatic expression may consist of a word or phrase that does not translate word for word into another language; for example, "the car was a lemon" has nothing to do with fruit, but rather, means that it did not run well and was a bad purchase. Similarly, "he was feeling blue" means he was sad, not of a blue color.

Imagery. Figurative language that creates mental pictures (e.g., "the rose opened its petals to drink deeply as the raindrops cascaded down its throat").

Independent clause. *See* Clause, main.

Linking verb. *See* Verb, linking.

Main clause. *See* Clause, main.

Metaphor. Figurative language that uses one kind of object or idea to suggest a likeness or analogy to another, unlike item (e.g., *drowning in paperwork, a flower bowing to the sun*).

Modal auxiliary. An auxiliary or helping verb that does not change form by adding -*s* or -*ing* (e.g., *can, must, might, may, should, would, could, ought*).

Noun. A word used to name a person, place, thing, or idea (e.g., *man, San Francisco, elephant, freedom*).

Noun, abstract. A word naming an idea or concept that does not have physical characteristics (e.g., *peace, freedom, love*).

Noun, concrete. A word naming a person, place, or thing that has physical characteristics (e.g., *clown, house, elephant*).

Noun, proper. A word naming a particular person, place, or thing that requires capitalization (e.g., *Mr. Smith, San Francisco, the Hope Diamond*).

Noun clause. *See* Clause, noun.

Noun phrase. *See* Phrase, noun.

Number, cardinal. Number used in simple counting (e.g., *one, four, seven*).

Number, ordinal. Number used in ranking (e.g., *first, fourth, seventh*).

Ordinal number. *See* Number, ordinal.

Parallel structure. Items in a series may consist of words, phrases, or clauses, but to create parallelism, all items in the series must use the same structure. For instance, "The tour stopped in Rome, Paris, and Amsterdam" creates a parallel noun series. "The campers were forced to cross the stream, hike up a hill, and build a campsite before resting" creates a parallel series of verb-object phrases. "The girls giggled, the boys laughed, and all were happy" creates a parallel series of independent or main clauses.

Participial phrase. A phrase using either the past or present participle of a verb to describe a noun or pronoun (e.g., "*Tired from working all morning,* Sam took a nap"; "*Leaping to her rescue,* Superman saved the girl").

Participle. A word that acts as either a verb or an adjective, depending on its use in the sentence. In "The ticking clock kept me awake," *ticking* is a present participle used as an adjective to describe the clock, but in "The clock was ticking loudly," the present participle is part of the verb phrase *was ticking.* Participles are either past or present. Present participles end in *-ing*; past participles end in *-ed, -d, -t, -en, -n (talked, loved, felt, taken, been).*

Person. Pronouns and verbs must agree in person and number (see first-person pronoun/verb, second-person pronoun/verb, third-person pronoun/verb).

Personification. Figurative language that gives human characteristics or qualities to a thing or abstraction (e.g., *the flower raised its face to take in the sun*).

Phrase. A group of related words, as in a prepositional phrase, a noun phrase, or a verb phrase.

Phrase, noun. A group of words related to a noun (e.g., *the fluffy, long-haired, Persian cat*).

Phrase, prepositional. A group of words beginning with a preposition and ending with its object (e.g., *into the deep, dark forest*).

Phrase, verb. A group of words including a main verb and one or more auxiliary or helping verbs (e.g., *has played, will be coming, should have paid*). A verb phrase may also include the object of the verb and describing words (e.g., *has played the game well, will be coming home soon, should have paid his bill more promptly*).

Preposition. A word used to show the relationship of a noun or pronoun to some other word in the sentence (e.g., *about, above, across, after, against*). (See Lesson 23 for a more complete list of prepositions.)

Prepositional phrase. *See* Phrase, prepositional.

Present participle. *See* Participle.

Relative clause. A subordinate or dependent clause beginning with a relative pronoun (*who, whom, whose, which, what, that*) (e.g., "He is a man *who doesn't fear anything*).

Second-person pronoun/verb. The verb in a sentence must agree with the person of the subject of the sentence; that is, a second-person singular subject (*you*) must use a second-person singular verb (*are, have, like,* etc.). *Note:* the second-person plural is the same as the singular.

Sentence. A group of words expressing a complete thought and using a subject and a predicate. A simple sentence contains just one independent clause. A compound sentence contains two independent clauses joined with a coordinate conjunction. A complex sentence contains one independent or main clause and one dependent or subordinate clause joined by a subordinate conjunction.

Sequence, logical. Order of items or parts determined by step-by-step logic.

Sequence, nonlinear. Order of items or parts that do not follow a step-by-step approach.

Series, items in. At least three items (words, phrases, or clauses) joined with commas and a conjunction (e.g., "I like *candy, ice cream, and cake*").

Simile. A comparison of two things using *like* or *as* (e.g., "The thunder sounded *like* drums in the distance, her hair is *as* gold *as* the sun").

Simple sentence. *See* Sentence.

Subjunctive mood. One of three moods in English (indicative, imperative, subjunctive) used mainly in two ways: (1) to express a condition contrary to fact (after *if* or *as though*) and (2) to express a wish. It applies mainly to the use of *were* in these two instances (e.g., "If I *were* taller, I could see over the crowd better" [condition contrary to fact]; "I wish I *were* taller" [expression of a wish]).

Subordinate clause. *See* Clause, subordinate.

Syllabication. Division of words into separately pronounced parts or syllables, for example, *syl-la-bi-ca-tion* has five syllables.

Synonym. A word with the same, or almost the same, meaning as another word (e.g., *lady/woman, ocean/sea*).

Theme. A central idea relating the parts of a piece of writing.

Thesis. The main idea or subject.

Third-person pronoun/verb. The verb in a sentence must agree with the person of the subject of the sentence; that is, a third-person singular subject (*he, she, it*) must use a third-person singular verb (*is, has, likes*, etc.). A third-person plural subject (*they*) must use a third-person plural verb (*are, have, like*, etc.).

Verb. A word that expresses action or a state of being (e.g., "The boy *threw* the ball," "The girl *is* pretty").

Verb, auxiliary. Accompanying verb, also called a *helping verb*, to show tense or negation (e.g., "I *have* been away all summer"; "I *do* not like broccoli").

Verb, linking. A verb that expresses a state of being rather than an action (e.g., "He *felt* sick"; "The apple *tasted* rotten"; "The boy *was* handsome"). Linking verbs include *appear, be, become, feel, grow, look, remain, seem, smell, sound, stay, taste.* Some of these verbs may also be active verbs, however. For instance, *The boy tasted the apple* shows action, whereas *The apple tasted rotten* shows a state of being.

Verb phrase. *See* Phrase, verb.

Index

The numbers following the entries are *lesson* numbers, not page numbers.